Elder Futhark Bindrunes

A Beginners Guide to Creating Bindrunes
+ Manifesting & Intention-Setting with Purpose

J.C. Marco

© Copyright – J.C. Marco 2021 – All rights reserved.
ISBN: 9798490097662

The content of this book may not be reproduced, duplicated, or transmitted without direct written permission from the author or the publisher.
Under no circumstances will any blame or legal responsibility be held against the publisher, or author, for any damages, reparation, or monetary loss due to the information contained within this book. Either directly or indirectly. You are responsible for your own choices, actions, and results.

Legal Notice:
This book is copyright protected. This book is only for personal use. You cannot amend, distribute, sell, use, quote, or paraphrase any part, or the content within this book, without the consent of the author or publisher.

Disclaimer Notice:
Please note the information contained within this document is for educational and entertainment purposes only. All effort has been executed to present accurate, up-to-date, reliable, and complete information. However, no warranties of any kind are declared or implied. Readers acknowledge that the author is not engaging in the rendering of legal, financial, medical, or professional advice. The content within this book has been derived from various sources. Please consult a licensed professional before attempting any techniques outlined in this book.
By reading this document, the reader agrees that under no circumstances is the author responsible for any losses, direct or indirect, which are incurred as a result of the use of the information contained within this document, including, but not limited to, — errors, omissions, or inaccuracies.

Welcome

Please take a moment to leave your review on Amazon. It is greatly appreciated, and it will help others like you find and enjoy this book. Many Blessings.

TABLE OF CONTENTS

- Introduction 1
- What are Runes? 4
- What are Bindrunes? 9
- Types of Bindrunes 13
- Creating Free-Form Bindrunes 23
- Getting to know the Runes 27
  - Rune Meanings & Symbols 29-32
- Adding Elemental Energy 35
- Adding Zodiac Energy 42
  - Zodiac Meanings & Symbols 45-46
- Manifesting with Purpose 51
- Setting your Intentions 52
  - Creating a Gratitude Loop 64
- Choosing Runes to Match your Intent ... 68
  - Three Circle Method 70
- Combining the Runes 76
- Looking for Hidden Runes 83
- Looking for Reversed Runes 91
  - Reversed Runes Meanings & Symbols ... 94-95
- Making Final Adjustments 102
- Completing & Finalizing your Bindrune ... 109
- Selecting the Material for your Bindrune ... 113
  - Material Correspondences 116
- The Creation Ritual 129
- Activating your Bindrune 136
- Using your Bindrune 156
- Conclusion 159
- Hidden & Reversed Rune Solutions ... 169
- Sources 172-174

Introduction

Have you ever wanted something so bad in your life that you would 'wish upon a star' or 'ask the universe' in the form of a prayer or ritual? Manifesting what we truly desire in our lives has become a norm in society today. We are constantly searching for new and better ways to strengthen our spiritual connection with the earth and universe.

Runes provide deeper insight and knowledge into the unanswered questions that we may encounter throughout our lives, but you may or may not be aware that there is a deeper side to the Elder Futhark Runes.

Bindrunes are a way to use the Elder Futhark to strengthen your spellwork, intentions, and manifesting desires. When making your bindrunes, many consider this a magickal process rather than a 'ritualized' form of practice where there is a definite start and stop.

The magickal process extends far beyond the creation, activation, and usage of your bindrune. It creates a dominant focal point to concentrate your will and desire, as this involves your energy and concentration throughout the entire process. This focus will help to manifest positive change in your life for days, weeks, months, and years to come.

Elder Futhark Bindrunes was written with the beginner in mind, goes over the most common design concepts, and teaches you how to create bindrunes that are as unique and powerful as you.

Everyone wants to have a better life full of joy and happiness, so consider this your roadmap to achieving success. Unfortunately, we sometimes get so caught up in our day-to-day lives that we forget the most critical factor in manifesting positive change — ourselves.

Taking the initiative and action towards a better life can be scary, but it is that first step that will get the universe's attention. Throughout this book, you will learn how to set your intentions, utilize elemental and astrological energetic influences, create powerful bindrunes, and manifest your desires with purpose.

We all want to live a more fulfilling and joyful life; we just keep forgetting that all we have to do is ask for it. Trusting in the universe seems to be a tall order, but we are all made up of the same universal energy and vibrations.

Are you ready to take action towards the life you want and go on a magickal adventure while doing it? I don't know about you, but I got some stuff that I want to change in my life, so let's make a cosmic phone call, shall we?

> "Whether you think you can or think you can't, either way you are right."
>
> Henry Ford

What are Runes?

The Elder Futhark is the most widely used runic language today. With their insight and knowledge, the runes can be used as a way to 'look into the future,' like reading a tarot card spread. Being the first complete adaptation of the alphabet in the 5th Century A.D., the runes have over fifteen centuries of history and mystery linked to them.

The origins of the runes used in Northern Europe by the Germanic people have been widely debated. Scholars worldwide have not found a conclusive match to any other particular writing system that would precisely tell them where the runic language has stemmed from.

The closest possibility to understanding where the runes originated from has been believed to be derived from the Etruscan alphabet, which, as some of you may know, became the Latin alphabet that most Western and English languages use to some extent today.

The runic languages or systems are commonly specified as 'runic alphabets,' which has become a widely accepted term for most people. However, in the Hebrew and Greek linguistic structures, alphabet comes from 'alpha' and 'beta,' which are the first two letters of these alphabets.

If you have a general knowledge of the runes, you will know that Elder Futhark does not start with the letters A and B. Instead, the first two letters are F and U, which could lead to some interesting problems.

I don't know about you, but if I was seeking answers from an ancient runic alphabet and the first two letters said F U, I would doubt whether or not they could do the job they are meant to do. So, when I started practicing with the runes, I didn't know if I should be offended that the runes told me to Eff Off right from the start!

All joking aside, the runes have blessed me with guidance, insight, knowledge, and wisdom over the years, and I hope you can trust in them as much as I do.

The name Futhark is derived from the first six runes in this 'alphabet.' Fehu (F), Urus (U), Thurizas (Th), Ansuz (A), Raido (R), and Kanu (C, K) spelling the word FUTHARK in succession when looking at the order of the runic alphabet from the beginning.

Their letter correspondences spell out FUTHARK, but the pronunciation can also be determined by the sound associations of each of these runes.

The word 'rune' translates from the Germanic, Old Irish Gaelic, Welsh, and Old English dialects, meaning 'secret,' 'mystery,' or 'miracle.'

The Elder Futhark runes are divided equally into three groups of eight runes each. Each of these groupings is called an Aett (pronounced eye-t or ight), an Icelandic and Norwegian term meaning family or clan. The three Aett's are Freyr's Aett, Heimdall's Aett, and Tyr's Aett. Each one is named after their respective Norse God or Goddess.

As we will mainly focus on getting to know the Elder Futhark Runes a little deeper throughout this book, another runic alphabet worth mentioning is called the Younger Futhark. The Younger Futhark Runes are a more condensed and compact version of the alphabet, and they were more commonly used in the Viking Age and only consisted of sixteen characters.

Along with the Elder Futhark, which is the most popular and widely used runic alphabet still to this day, many other runic alphabets have been utilized throughout the ages. Some of the different runic alphabets include, but are not limited to, Anglo-Saxon runes, Marcomannic runes, Younger Futhark, Medieval runes, and Dalecarlian runes.

Because runes are an ancient language, the practice is often shrouded in mystery. There may be many different interpretations of the meanings associated with each rune. Nevertheless, the runes, their symbols, and translations have been derived from many years of history, and today, thousands of people have come to know and trust the information passed down through the ages.

What are Bindrunes?

Bindrunes are precisely how it sounds. The 'binding' of two or more runes that are overlaid and connected to create an amulet, talisman or sigil for manifestation, intention-setting, and magickal purposes.

In the age of Viking inscriptions, which were typically found as wood or stone carvings, seeing bindrunes were relatively rare. In most cases, when they were discovered, they were simply a way to display the carver's name, or they only served as 'ornamental' decoration with no real magickal meaning associated with them.

In Iceland, it was later discovered in the 1600s that bindrunes were being used in medieval manuscripts with magickal intentions and purposes linked to them. One notable example would be from the famous Icelandic staves or Galdrastafir, which shows the Vegvisir and the Helm of Awe, combinations of runes (bindrunes) with magickal purposes and intentions.

VIKING AND ICELANDIC DEFINITIONS

Staves: a vertical wooden post or plank in a building or other structure.

Galdrastafir [gal-draw-sta-fur]: Icelandic word for 'magickal staves.' These Galdrastafir are sigils that were credited to have supposed magickal effects. These staves have been in various Icelandic Grimoires (books) dating back to the 17th century and later.

Vegvisir [v-egg-viz-ear]: Icelandic word for 'signpost' or 'wayfinder,' is a magickal stave used to help the bearer find their way through rough weather or storms. The Vegvisir is also known as the 'runic compass,' made of eight Viking rune staves, and is also utilized as a symbol of protection and guidance.

Helm of Awe: Arguably the most famous Vegvisir or Galdrastafir, the Helm of Awe (as seen with the circle of runes on the cover of this book) is an excellent example of the typical 'runic compass' that the Vikings used. The Helm of Awe was believed to invoke protection from the ancient Norse Gods.

Also known as the 'Helm of Terror,' this Vegvisir is most notably mentioned in poetic Norse stories where the dragon Fafnir is said to attribute his power to the Helm of Awe. This symbol is said to be one of the most powerful in Norse Mythology, simply because of how strong the dragon Fafnir was in protecting and keeping everyone away from his ill-gotten riches.

It is also believed that Icelandic warriors would put this symbol on their clothing to invoke the strength and fierce energy of the dragon when in battle. It was also suggested that the Helm of Awe was used to bring fear to enemies, just as the dragon Fafnir paralyzed his foes with fear before striking.

The stories behind the Helm of Awe are genuinely fascinating. If you are enthralled by Norse mythology and culture, I encourage you to read more about this powerful ancient symbol, as I could write most of the book on this mythological story alone.

Bindrunes are gaining traction and popularity again in modern culture, and many practitioners and Norse believers use them to cast spells. They are also used as amulets and sigils for manifestation and intention-setting work. By combining different runes, you ask for a result from the gods — good or bad — for you, a loved one, or maybe a friend.

Before we get into the process of how to choose your runes, I will go over the general designs and most commonly used design instructions to create your bindrunes.

Throughout the book, you will also see many note pages which you can use. Please feel free to write down and utilize these pages for information you have learned, personal notes or doodle pages.

Types of Bindrunes

When creating your bindrunes, there are many different ways to make a symbol that works best for your intentions. Everyone has a particular method or a unique set of rules for creating bindrunes. Do not feel pressured into following specific 'instructions' as everyone is different. Do what feels right and what works best for you.

Feel free to explore and get creative with the runes. The bindrunes are connected to your energy, with your manifesting and intention desires at the core of its power.

If you are an individual who likes to follow specific 'instructions,' the following types of bindrunes will most likely be right up your alley. These are the basic guidelines for 'structured' bindrunes, which are commonly used.

LINEAR BINDRUNE

A linear bindrune is simply two or more runes combined along one uniform linear axis or line, vertically top to bottom. Linear bindrunes can also be divided into two individual types as described below:

- STACKED

Commonly used in spells to manifest a reality.

A stacked bindrune is the easiest, minimally complex, and most common. These bindrunes are created using two — rarely three — different runes. The most famous example of this type of bindrune can be seen on almost every electronic device in the modern world today. Most likely, you have seen this bindrune yourself. It is the everyday 'Bluetooth' symbol.

Yes, this simple yet effective symbol for the fantastic feature that allows you to connect multiple devices and share information comes from bindrune origins and Norse mythology.

The two runes that have been combined to produce the famous 'Bluetooth' logo are the initials of Harald Bluetooth. Bluetooth was the nickname for a Danish King named Harald Gormsson, who lived in Denmark around the middle of the 10th century.

He was the one that is credited for unifying the Danes into one kingdom and making them Christians, as inscribed on the Jelling Stone in the town of Jelling, Denmark. In 1996, multiple tech companies were working on new technology, but each had a different name. Finally, the companies agreed to meet in one central location, which happened to be in the community of Lund in Sweden.

The special interest group took inspiration from the king's nickname and decided to call their new technology 'Bluetooth.'

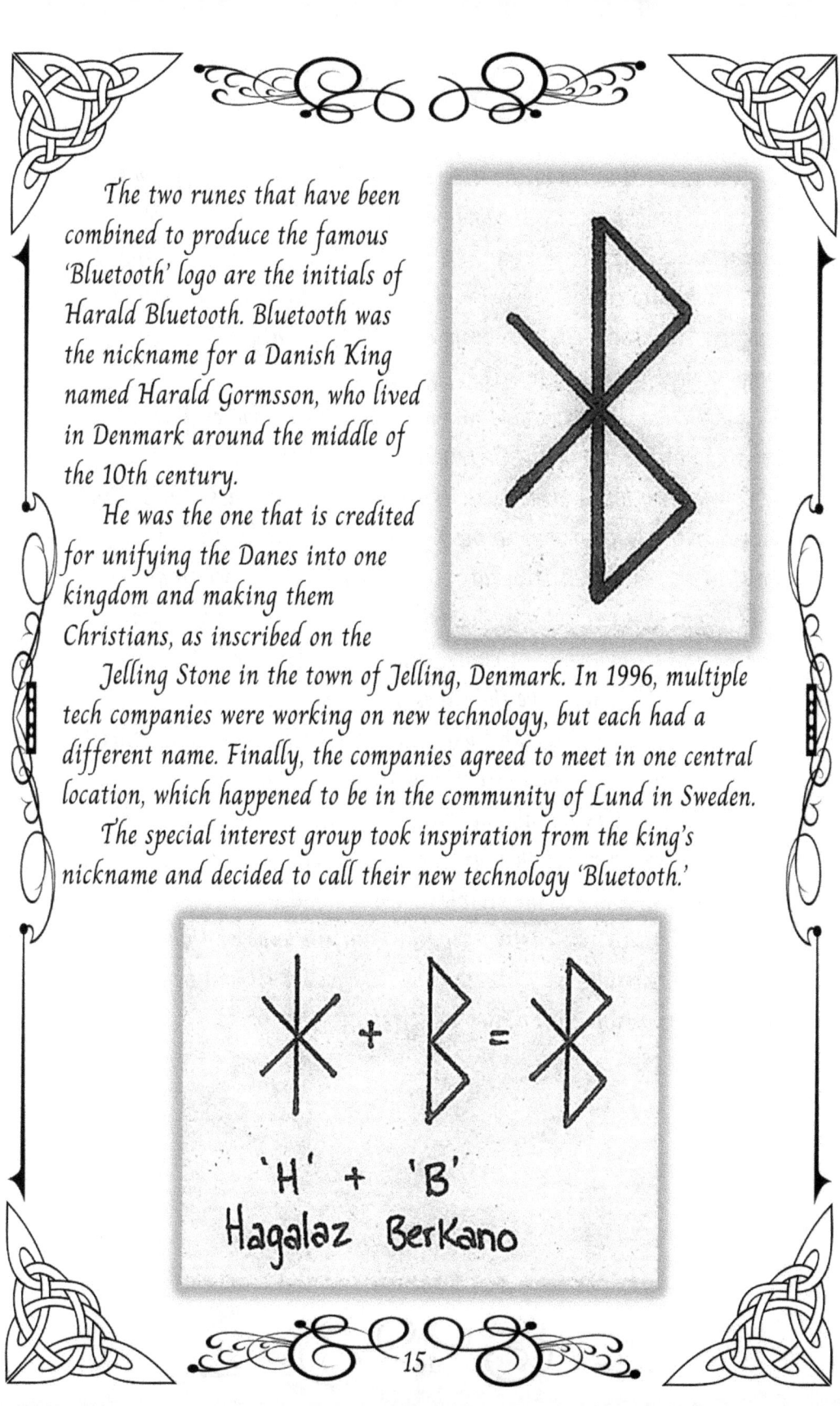

The runes signifying the letters 'H' and 'B' are derived from the Younger Futhark runic alphabet, which only consisted of sixteen characters during the Viking Age. It wasn't until the Elder Futhark runes were later re-discovered and interpreted that the entirety of the alphabet could be translated from each of the twenty-four individual runes, except for the letters Q, V, and X.

Today, many individuals who practice with the runes associate an existing rune to one of the three unassociated letters. For X, this could be Gebo, which has a large X as its runic symbol, but associates with the letter G. Most commonly, the X is also associated with Thurizas, which is the rune that translates to 'Th' when used in writing (**Th**eology). Q is typically associated with Kanu, which translates to C and K. And if you write in runes, and come across the letter V, Wunjo (W) or Fehu (F) tend to be the runes most commonly used.

Once you feel comfortable using the runes more often and start to memorize them, you could essentially assign each of the three unassociated letters to any one rune that suits your style. Just be mindful of which runes they are, or a secret letter or note might be somewhat confusing to the recipient. You may also notice that the letter E is greedy and has two separate runes: Eywas and Ehwaz. So, feel free to reassign one of those runes as you see fit, but be mindful that these two runes are radically different in meaning.

- SAME-STAVE

Commonly used in spells and magick to attack a problem.

The same-stave bindrune is most commonly associated with Scandinavian Runic inscriptions. This type of rune combines multiple different runes along a vertical line, or axis and is generally separated to distinguish each one individually.

Using the Elder Futhark runes and my name J.C. Marco as an example, let's see what my same-stave bind rune would look like:

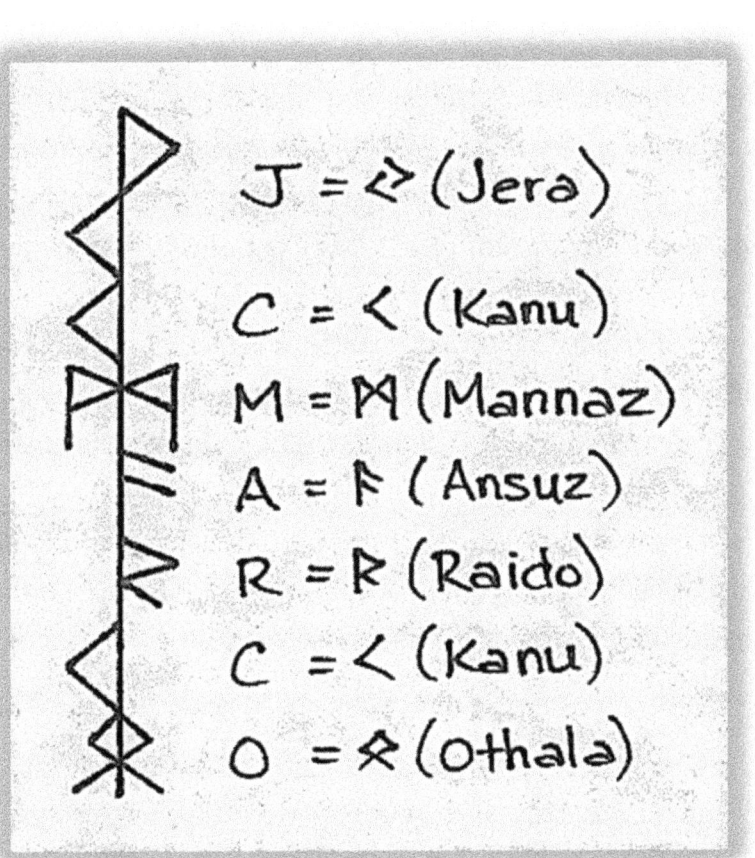

- RADIAL OR STAVE

Commonly used in defense spells and protection amulets.

The best way to know if your bindrune is radial would be its circular design with multiple 'staves' stemming from one central point. As mentioned earlier, the Helm of Awe is a perfect example of a radial bindrune.

Your radial bindrune can be a simple four-pointed cross, or it can be as complex as the Helm of Awe and have up to eight or more points if you like. I have created another example using my name to show you how a structured radial bind rune would look.

I chose to go with the eight-pointed 'star' so that each letter of my name will have one stave. The following example shows how I would interpret my name into a radial bind rune. There is one stave extra if you also notice, so I decided to add the rune Daegaz, which means Harmony or Success.

I have simply associated my name with Harmony or Success and created a powerful radial bindrune. Alternatively, I could add a zodiac or elemental symbol to the extra stave to increase the energy within this bindrune.

I can now carve, paint, sew, or draw this personal bindrune on the material of my choice to always have with me, so I am constantly in sync with my intentions and manifesting energies.

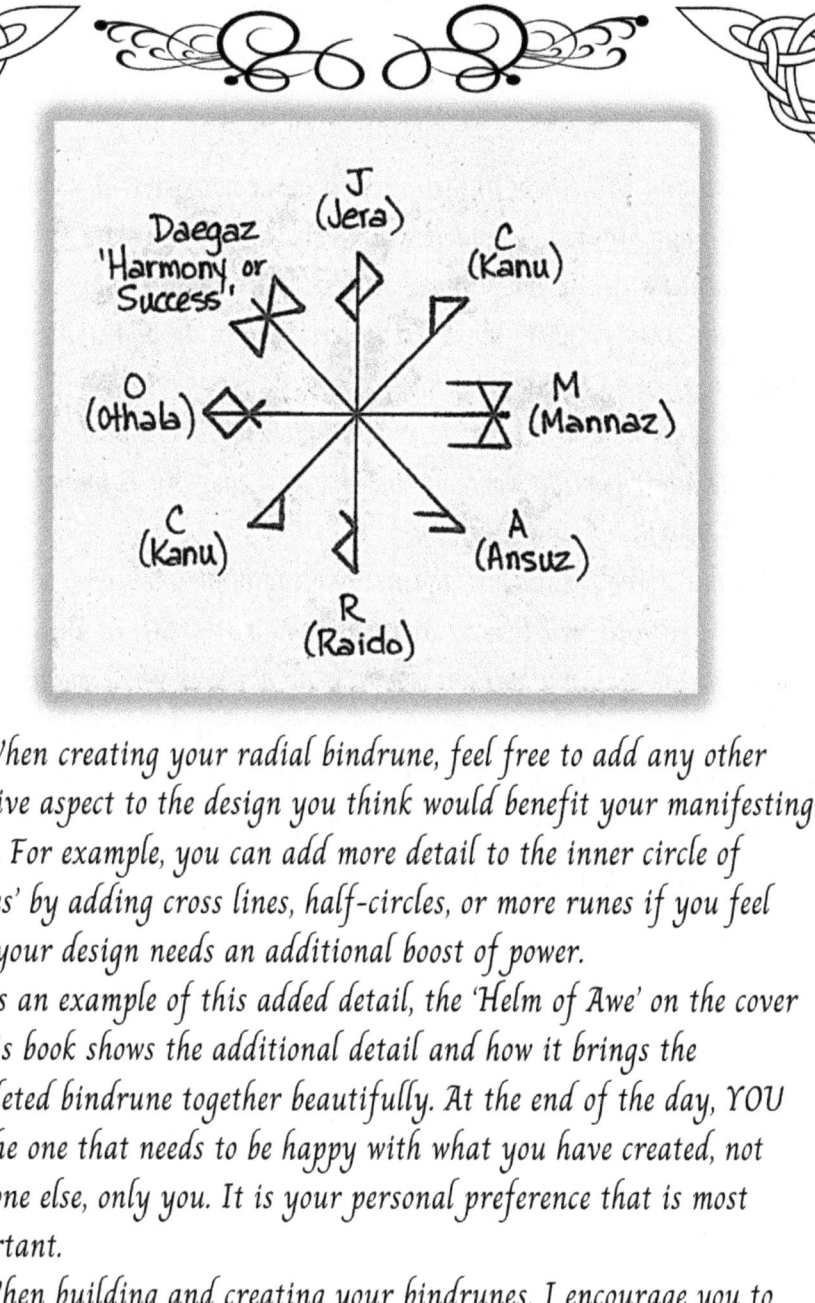

When creating your radial bindrune, feel free to add any other creative aspect to the design you think would benefit your manifesting goals. For example, you can add more detail to the inner circle of 'staves' by adding cross lines, half-circles, or more runes if you feel that your design needs an additional boost of power.

As an example of this added detail, the 'Helm of Awe' on the cover of this book shows the additional detail and how it brings the completed bindrune together beautifully. At the end of the day, YOU are the one that needs to be happy with what you have created, not someone else, only you. It is your personal preference that is most important.

When building and creating your bindrunes, I encourage you to try the linear, try the stacked, try the same-stave, and try the radial with the same runes for each design. One design might stand out more to you than the others, and when you see the 'right one,' you will know.

Practicing with these guidelines will build your confidence in creating your bindrunes, and it will become easier to create one on the fly if needed quickly. We all have stressful days, and if you can create a bindrune in a pinch to manifest inner peace in an aggravating situation, then go for it. Why not?

Just a gentle reminder that if you follow a Wiccan path, keep in mind the all-important verse of the Wiccan Rede: "An it harm none, do what ye will."

I would strongly suggest against making bindrune amulets or talismans with ill-will toward another human or creature. But, then again, that is only my opinion. There is no black or white magick. It is both because nature is both, and the true intentions lie in the practitioner's heart. So, essentially, do whatever you choose and follow the path that feels right for you; just brace yourself for any potential consequences or karmic backlash.

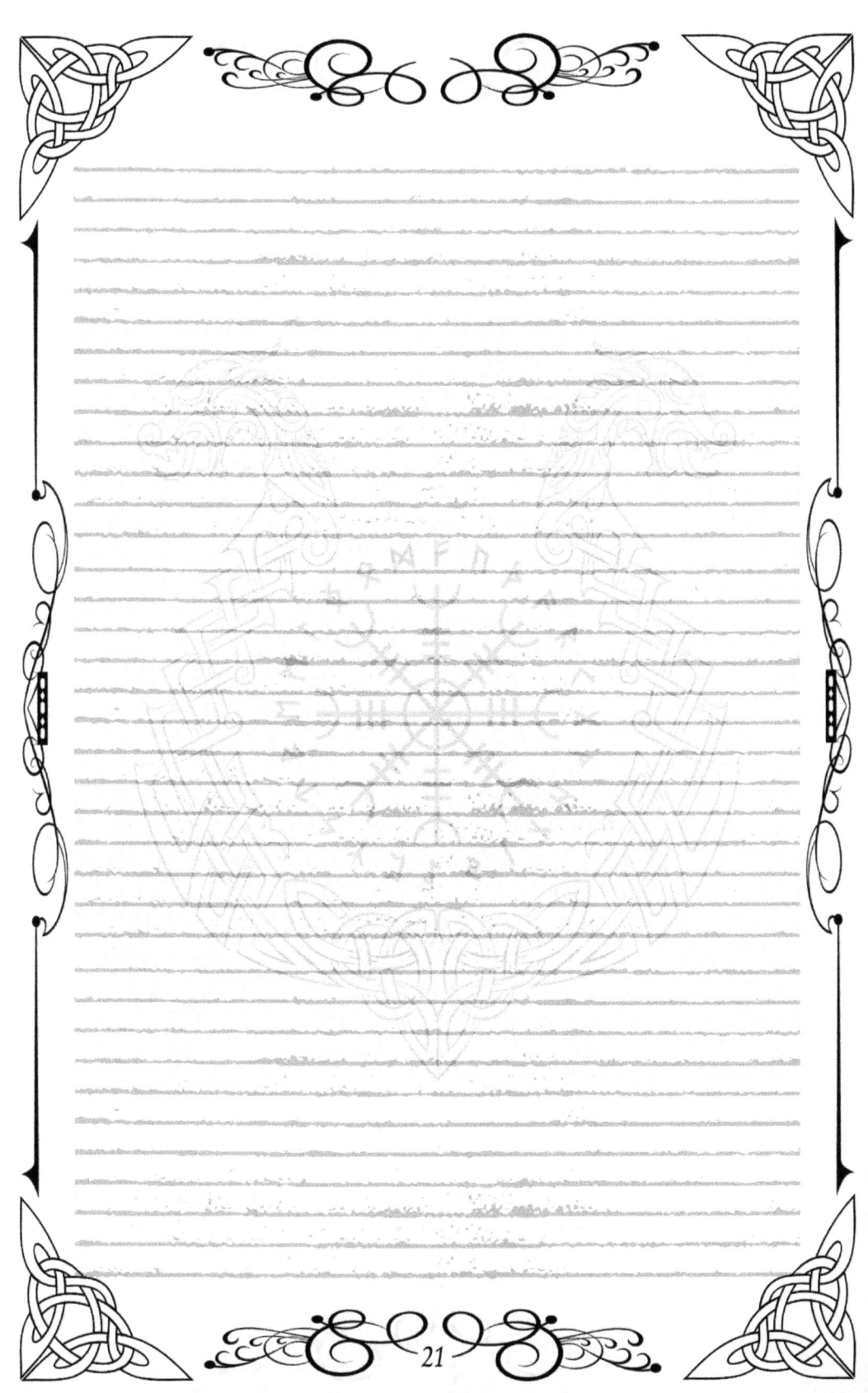

Creating Free-Form Bindrunes

Now that we have covered the basic design 'templates,' let's dive into the fun and excitement of creating your very own bindrunes from scratch. This method gives you complete creative control over the look and feel of how your bindrune will turn out. In my opinion, this is the best way to construct a bindrune because you get to doodle and try different designs.

Once you have chosen the runes you would like to include in your design (which we will go over in the "Getting to Know the Runes" and "Setting your Intentions" chapters), grab a pencil, a piece of paper, and an eraser. Since all the runes comprise straight lines, having a ruler on hand would be a handy tool to use.

When you are in your creative zone, I found that it is easier to have each of the runes you have chosen drawn out separately at the top of your worksheet or page, helping you reference each one when combining them.

Typically, you would have multiple pages and choices of different combinations that you have drawn. It is up to you and how you feel about each design to decide on the bindrune that calls out to you.

For simplicity sake, I have only provided four bindrune examples for us to review together. I have chosen to use Fehu, Wunjo, and Berkana as the three runes I will be binding together in this example.

FEHU **WUNJO** **BERKANA**
PROSPERITY SUCCESS NEW BEGINNINGS

Now that we have chosen our runes, this is when you can open your mind and let your creativity come to fruition. Start by drawing the runes together in as many combinations as you can. The goal is to create a bindrune energetically connected to your intentions for manifesting what you want in your life.

With the three runes I have chosen, these are the different combinations that I came up with:

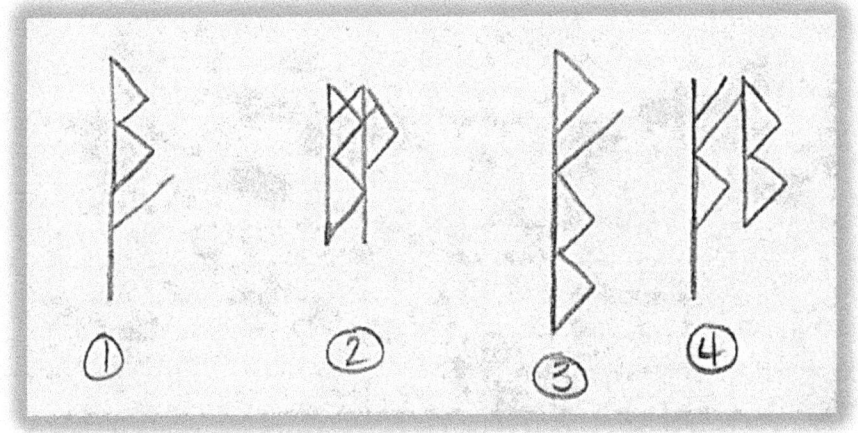

Can you see the three individual runes in each? It's pretty easy to come up with multiple combinations, and that is a good thing. The more creative you get when binding your chosen runes together, the better chance you will find the design that speaks to you and embodies your manifesting intentions.

I like 2 & 4. What do you think?

_____
_____
_____
_____

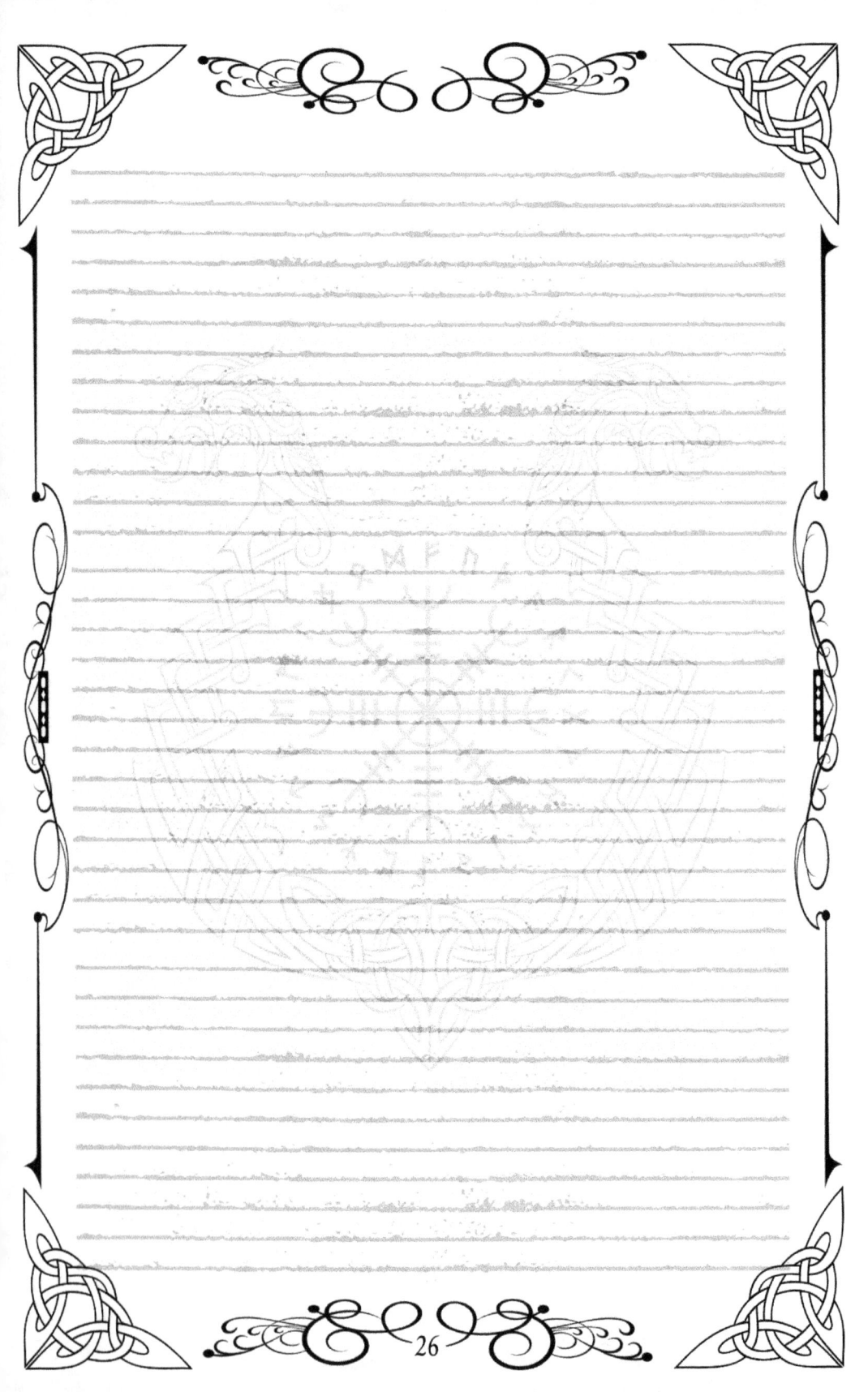

Getting to know the Runes

When working with the runes, the first step is to study and understand what their meanings are. Knowing what each rune means will help you gain a deeper understanding when you combine the runes to create your powerful amulet or talisman.

This can be an intimidating step, especially for someone who is just beginning or has no idea what the runes are all about. However, I assure you that you have nothing to fear. Try not to let this crucial step deter you from beginning your magickal workings and manifesting.

The more you understand and know, the more improved and more powerful your bindrunes will become over time. But, at the same time, do not be intimidated or afraid to the point that you start to feel overwhelmed and creatively paralyzed.

Practice makes perfect, and the first step in becoming successful with bindrunes is to take that leap of faith and start practicing as much as possible. You don't have to jump right into the deep end and begin with a complicated bindrune design. Instead, start simple and only choose a two-rune sigil or talisman that can be created to manifest a short-term goal.

Over time you will start to become more and more comfortable creating your bindrunes, and as you progress, the complexity and intricacy of your designs will also improve.

There are many different runic alphabets that we can choose from to study and understand, so it would be easier to focus on only one. However, since the Elder Futhark is still the most popular today, used by beginners and experienced rune users alike, let us get you better acquainted with their meanings and symbols.

FEHU "fay-who" - *Cattle or Wealth*
Letter Association: F
Meaning: Cattle, prosperity, some sort of gain, fulfillment, wealth, material needs, goals, promotion.

URUS or URUZ "oo-rooze" - *Auroch or Wild Ox*
Letter Association: U
Meaning: Strength, life force, determination, desire, inner feelings, water, rain, motivation, perseverance.

THURIZAS "thur-ee-saws" - *Thorn or Giant*
Letter Association: Th (<u>TH</u>ing)
Meaning: Giants, brutal force, unexpected change, hardship, pain, introspection, focus, danger, destruction or defense.

ANSUZ "awn-sooz" - *Discovery, Signs, Perception*
Letter Association: A
Meaning: Odin, communication, air, leadership, justice, teacher, intelligence, inspiration, wisdom, good advice.

RAIDO or RAIDHO "rye-though" - *Wagon or Chariot*
Letter Association: R
Meaning: Travel, movement, journey, change, destiny, horse, expanding your horizons, perspective, evolution.

KANU or KENAZ "cane-awes" - *Beacon or Torch*
Letter Association: C, K (Q)
Meaning: Fire, warmth, energy, power, positive attitude, knowledge, wisdom, insight, creativity, inspiration.

Remember earlier when I mentioned that the first six runes in the Elder Futhark are where the name was derived from originally? For example, look at the above runes and their 'Letter Association.' What does it spell?

GEBO "yee-boe" - *Gift*
Letter Association: G (X)
Meaning: Gift, partnership, commitment, love, marriage, generosity, bountiful blessings, balance.

WUNJO "woon-yo" - *Joy*
Letter Association: W (V)
Meaning: Joy, pleasure, harmony, kinship, success, lasting emotional happiness, recognition, contentment.

HAGALL or HAGALAZ "haw-gaw-laws" - *Hail*
Letter Association: H
Meaning: Limitations, delays, forces outside your control, disruption, destruction, change, loss, storm, air.

NAUTHIZ "now-theez" - *Restriction or Conflict*
Letter Association: N
Meaning: Patience, hardship, passing through a difficult learning situation, need, responsibility, frustration.

ISA "ee-saw" - *Ice*
Letter Association: I
Meaning: Plans on hold, frustrations, blocks, patience, stagnation, rest, challenge, pause, waiting.

JERA "yare-ah" - *Year or Good Harvest*
Letter Association: J, Y
Meaning: Harvest, reaping the rewards for past efforts, justice, change, cycle, motion, earth.

EYWAS "eye-was" - *Yew Tree*
Letter Association: E
Meaning: Endurance, achieving goals with resilience, junction, endings, transformation, rebirth, dreams, death.

PERTHRO "perth-row" - *Destiny, Secret, Feminine Fertility*
Letter Association: P
Meaning: Mystery, occult knowledge, coincidence, secrets uncovered, magick, prophecy, chance, work, sexuality.

ALGIZ "all-yeese" - *Elk or Protection*
Letter Association: Z
Meaning: Support, wisdom of the universe, protection, assistance, shield, manifesting your dreams.

SOWILO "soe-wee-low" - *The Sun*
Letter Association: S
Meaning: Victory, awareness, energy, strength, activity, male energy, consciousness, thunderbolt, honor.

TEIWAZ "tee-whaz" - *Authority and Confidence*
Letter Association: T
Meaning: Rationality, distinction, success in a competition, warrior strength, truth, duty, discipline, justice, struggle.

BERKANA or BERKANO "bear-kawn-oh" - *Fertility, Success*
Letter Association: B
Meaning: Birth, new beginnings, true home, growth, health, earth, birch tree, liberation.

EHWAZ "aye-waz" - *Horse*
Letter Association: E
Meaning: Movement, steady progress, physical shift, equality, duality, change, love, partnerships, twin forces.

MANNAZ "man-awes" - *Mankind*
Letter Association: M
Meaning: Interdependence, collective potential, self improvement, change, family, humanity.

LAGUZ "law-goose" - *Water or Lagoon*
Letter Association: L
Meaning: Evolution, cleansing, female figure, emotion, fears, water, sea, ocean.

INGWAZ "ing-goose" - *Inner Growth, Virtue, Home, Family*
Letter Association: NG (thiNG)
Meaning: Successful conclusion, relief, personal development, energy, sex, grounded, balance, work.

OTHALA "oath-awe-law" - *Heritage, Ancestral Property*
Letter Association: O
Meaning: Gift, legacy, spiritual growth, possessions, ancestral wisdom, home, goddess, moon, estate.

DAEGAZ or DAGAZ "daw-gawz" - *Day or Dawn*
Letter Association: D
Meaning: Increase, steady growth, awakening, happiness, success, time.

As you can see, there are multiple meanings for each rune. The most important factor when choosing the runes would be to examine all the definitions carefully. Everyone is a beginner at some point, and it can be a little overwhelming to see all the different explanations and interpretations.

Someone could effortlessly write an entire course that teaches how runes are understood and interpreted. Feel free to highlight all the words under each rune that stand out to you, so you have a visual shortcut to see all the available symbols that could work well for your bindrune.

After you have studied and gone through each meaning, look at the choices you have. Do you feel that you have too few or too many runes? Depending on the design you are going for, if you have too many runes, this could indicate that your thoughts are unfocused and unclear. On the other hand, if you think you have too few runes, there is potential that you have not considered all the possibilities that pertain to achieving your goal.

It will take some time and practice to find the balance between too many or too few runes. Start simple. Don't overcomplicate things. Take a deep breath, focus, and take your time; this is not a race.

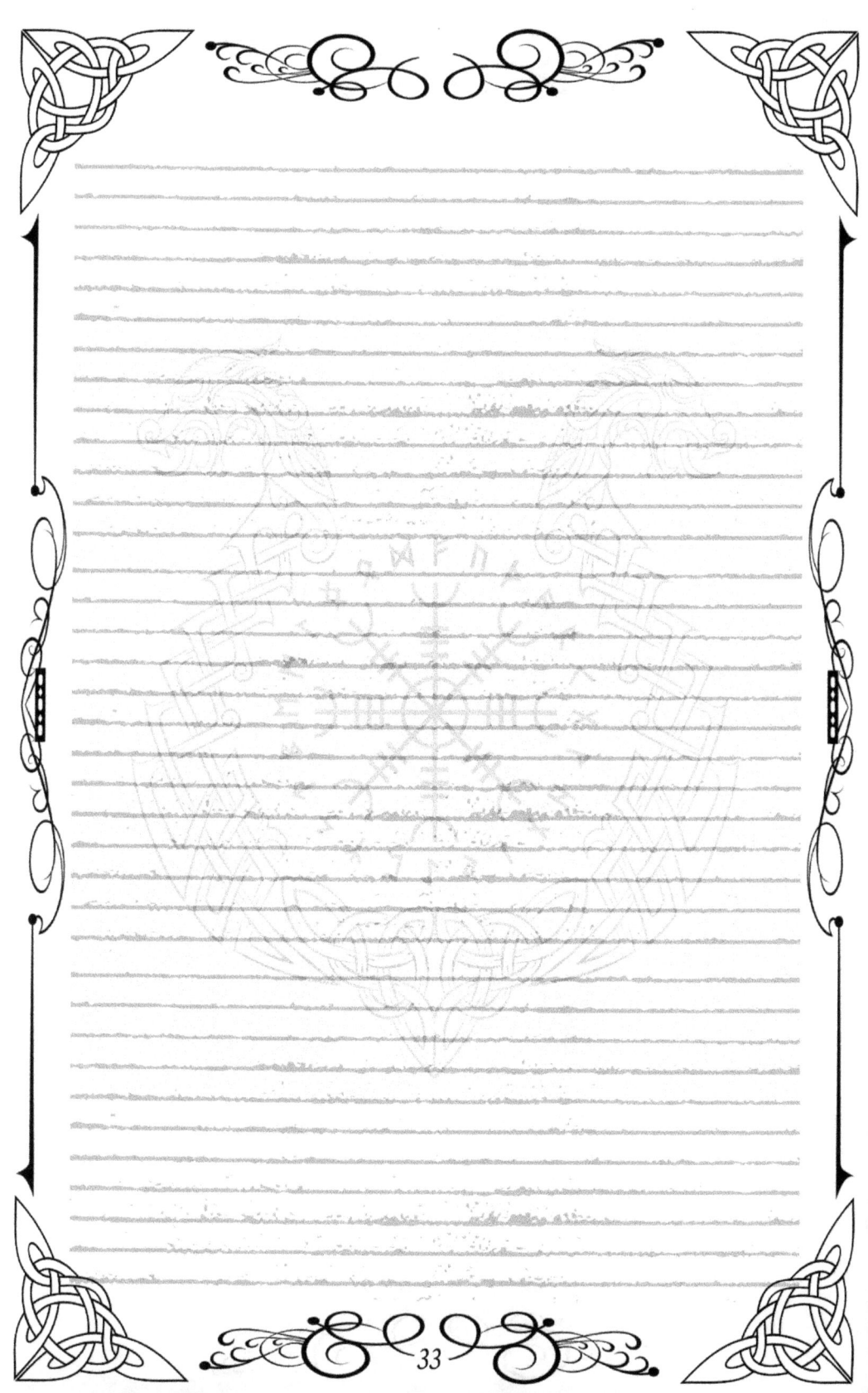

Adding Elemental Energy

Alongside the runes, which are influential symbols in and of themselves, you may wish to boost the power in your bindrune using elemental energy. Everything in nature comprises the four essential elements: Earth, Air, Fire, and Water.

Knowledge of these four essential elements will allow you to understand the laws of nature better, help you attain greater wisdom, happiness, power, and help to boost your manifesting desires. The energies and vibrations of the elements are intricately connected with the universe and having them on your side is a great asset.

Many people will tell you that there is a fifth element depending on your beliefs or spiritual path. There have been references in Hollywood which portrayed this additional element being the power of love. However, it is more commonly practiced and believed that spirit, metal, or wood is the fifth element.

Each of these seven elements has different meanings attached to them, just like the individual meanings of the runes. Therefore, you can use the elemental symbol that best embodies the manifesting desire you want to achieve.

I like to use the element associated with my zodiac sign because this is who I am, and the universe determined this powerful symbol on the day I was born. Therefore, granting me access to the most potent form of universal personal energy.

There are many different versions of what all five elements encompass. I will show you the four basic elemental symbols along with spirit, metal, and wood so you can decide how you would like to use them in your bindrunes.

[Elemental symbols chart: Earth, Air, Fire, Water, Spirit, Metal, Wood]

Below is a comprehensive list of each element's properties and correspondences to help you choose which symbol to include in your bindrune creation.

EARTH

Stability, feeling grounded, stillness, fertility, potential, cycles of life and death, thoughtfulness, trust, balance, abundance, beauty, honesty.

Zodiac Signs: *Taurus, Virgo, Capricorn*
Planets: *Saturn*
Season: *Winter*
Time of Day: *Midnight*
Color: *Green*
Direction: *North*
Gender: *Feminine (Passive)*
Elemental: *Gnomes*

AIR

Creativity, intelligence, new beginnings, compassion, courage, sadness, jealousy, responsibility, inner strength.

Zodiac Signs: Gemini, Libra, Aquarius
Planets: Jupiter
Season: Spring
Time of Day: Sunrise, Morning
Color: Yellow
Direction: East
Gender: Masculine (Active)
Elemental: Sylphs (Invisible beings)

FIRE

Strength, blood, life-force, protective, driving away darkness, purifying, honor, joy, sincerity, acceptance, creativity.

Zodiac Signs: Aries, Leo, Sagittarius
Planets: Sun, Mars
Season: Summer
Time of Day: Noon (Sun at its zenith)
Color: Red
Direction: South
Gender: Masculine (Active)
Elemental: Salamander

WATER

Intuition, emotion, intelligence, unconscious mind, gentleness, cautious, conservative.

> **Zodiac Signs:** Cancer, Scorpio, Pisces
> **Planets:** Moon, Venus
> **Season:** Fall or Autumn
> **Time of Day:** Sunset
> **Color:** Blue
> **Direction:** West
> **Gender:** Feminine (Passive)
> **Elemental:** Undines (water-based nymphs)

SPIRIT

Because spirit is not a 'physical' element like the others, it does not have the same list of correspondences. This 'element' is simply a bridge between the spiritual and physical, the body and soul, and physical and celestial realms. There are various resources available that will list associations for tools, planets, gender, etc. Still, this knowledge is less standardized and differentiates depending on the source where you find the information.

The circle is the most common symbol for spirit. Others may use the eight-spoked wheel (which would automatically make it a radial bindrune), or the spiral tends to be a favorite to represent spirit.

> **Direction:** Above, below, within
> **Colors:** Orange, White, Purple, Violet

METAL

Compassion, righteousness, courage, inner strength, responsibility, virtue, morality, focus. It is commonly associated with Air.

Zodiac Signs (Chinese): Monkey and Rooster
Planets: Venus
Season: Autumn
Time of Day: Morning
Color: White, Grey
Direction: West
Elemental: White Tiger

WOOD

Kindness, anger, decisiveness, ignorance, forgiveness, wisdom, freedom, change, growth, irritability, frustration.

Zodiac Signs (Chinese): Tiger and Rabbit
Planets: Jupiter
Season: Spring
Time of Day: Afternoon
Color: Green
Direction: East
Gender: Masculine
Elemental: Green Dragon

Feel free to use different formations using the various elemental symbols. You can use one, many, or none when creating your bindrune. The elements will add a definitive source of power and energy to the intentions that you are embedding into your design. If you feel that binding two parts together will be enough to manifest your desires, then go for it. Find what works for you and run with it.

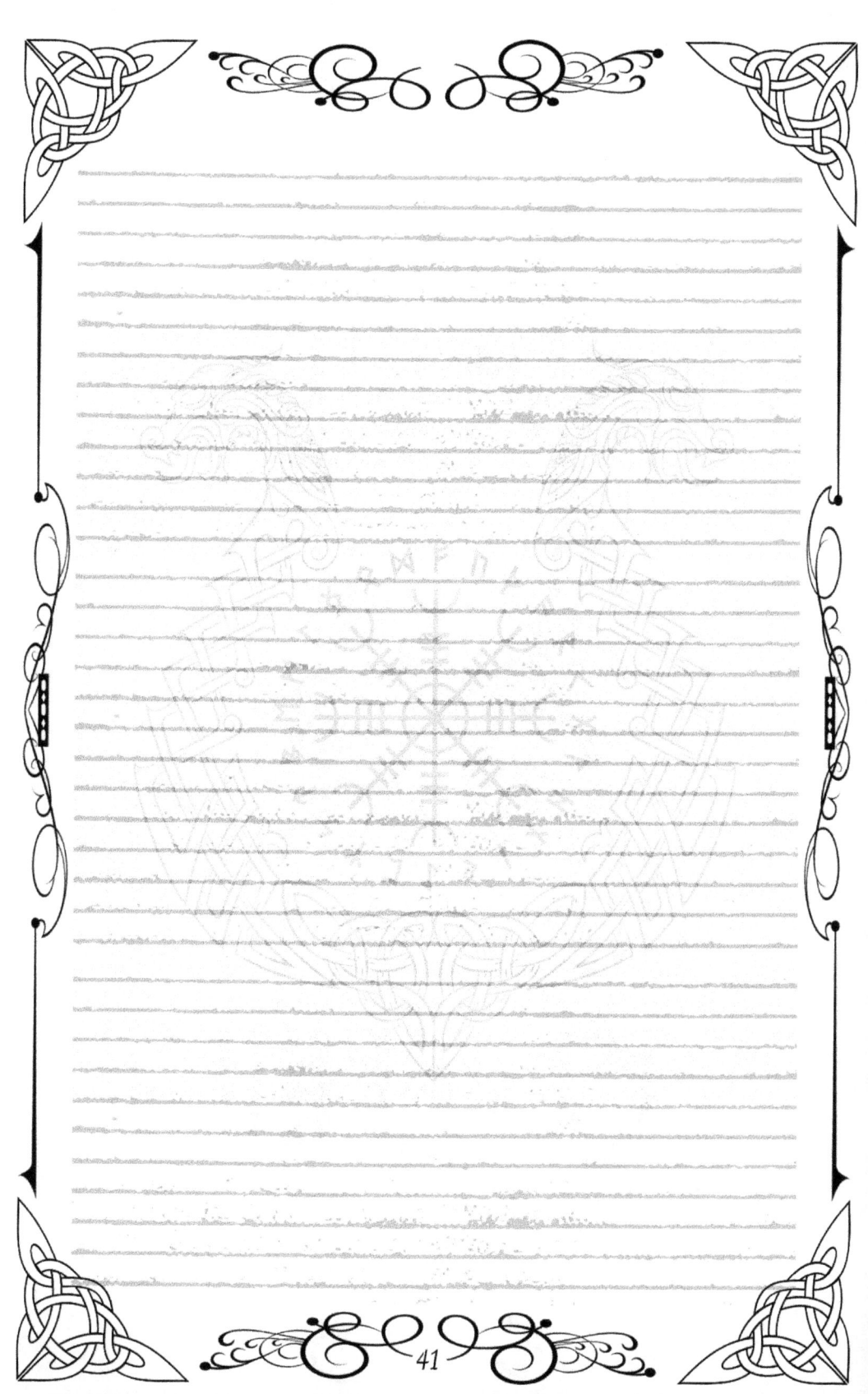

Adding Zodiac Energy

Your astrological sign, or zodiac, is a powerful symbol all by itself. Your zodiac was determined when you were born based on the location of the sun and the stars, and earth's precise position beneath them. Each of the twelve zodiacs has its grouping of stars in the night sky that make up a shape or picture called a constellation or 'star sign.'

Your zodiac sign is a great resource to help you understand personal strengths and weaknesses, traits, desires, your attitude toward life and other individuals, as well as your essential characteristics, fears, flaws, and preferences.

A great majority of the world's population are firm believers in astrology and tend to make choices and life decisions based on their daily horoscope. Furthermore, most people who read their horoscopes regularly find comfort, fulfillment, and a sense of satisfaction, because reading about what the stars are predicting for their life has a profound effect on individuals and the way they choose to live their lives.

The more knowledge we have about astrology and horoscopes, we notice that they are indeed very insightful and correct when associated with all the different aspects of our lives. In addition, the more we learn, the more apparent things become because our unique horoscopes can help us reveal our natural abilities and qualities and lets us know future obstacles and problems in advance.

If you desire to manifest a relationship of some sort, astrology is a great way to find out which zodiac signs you would be compatible with, and which ones would be conflicting. Knowledge of your love or relationship potential can positively impact your decisions and help you take advantage of opportunities, which can guide you into taking appropriate measures that would lead to a happy love or married life.

The insight, wisdom, and knowledge we get from astrology can also help us find a career or educational path. The effects of the stars and planets on our horoscopes can help guide us to a good and successful life.

Now imagine the power of combining your zodiac sign with its relative elemental sign in a bindrune. These two alone would bring you such passion and energy. With the vibrations of the universe and stars imbued within your zodiac sign, plus those of the elements and your chosen rune energies, you potentially have an enormously powerful amulet for manifesting anything you desire.

Most people already know what their zodiac sign is, but I will include all the symbols here for the sake of creating bindrunes. You may want to have the zodiac sign of a loved one, a family member, or a friend when making your bindrunes, and the easiest way to find out which one is theirs is to know their birthday.

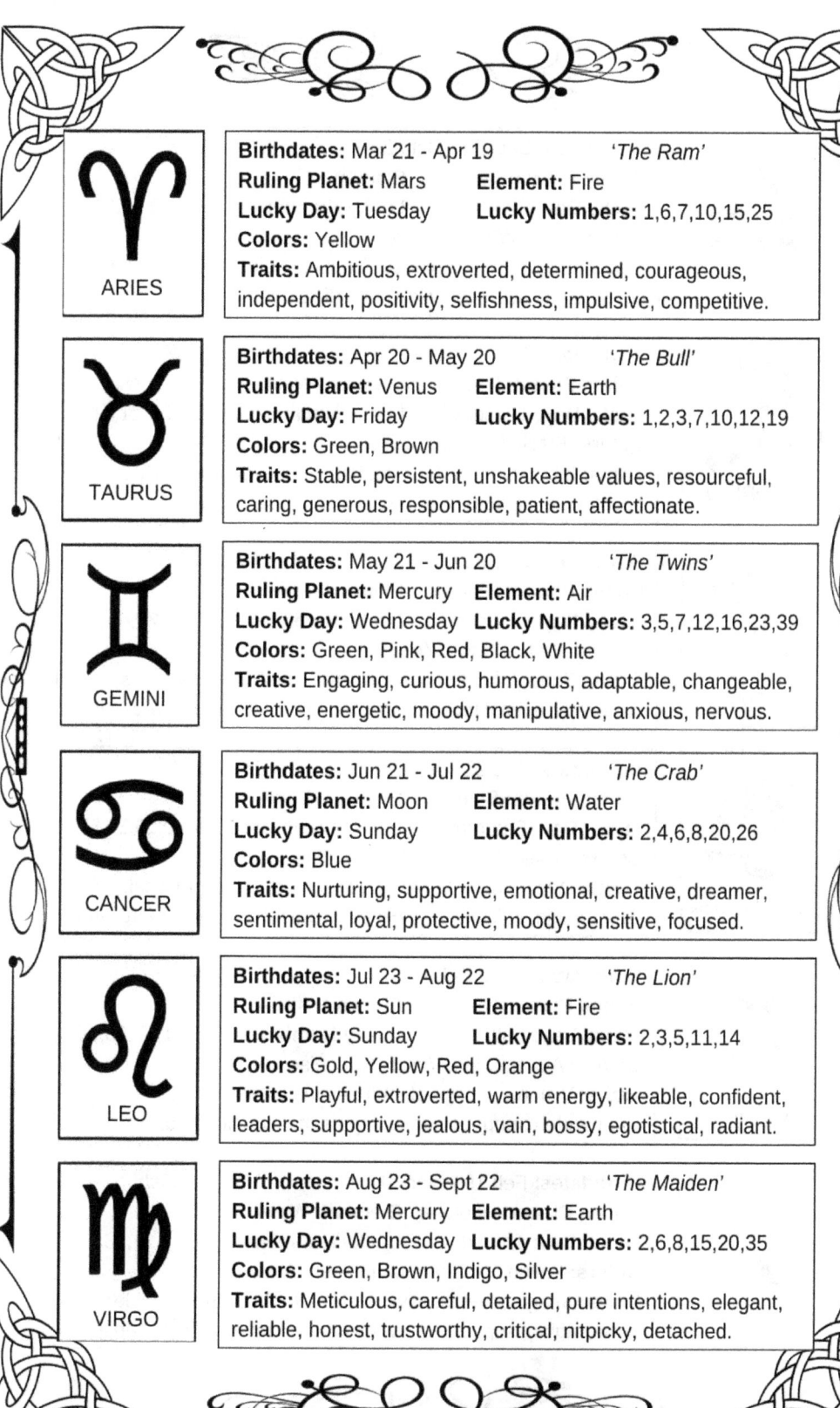

LIBRA
Birthdates: Sept 23 - Oct 22   'The Scales'
Ruling Planet: Venus   **Element:** Air
Lucky Day: Friday   **Lucky Numbers:** 1,5,6,7,10,14,24
Colors: Pink, White, Orange
Traits: Gracious, fair-minded, forgiving, relationship focused, considerate, laid-back, flirty, superficial, unpredictable, lazy.

SCORPIO
Birthdates: Oct 23 - Nov 21   'The Scorpion'
Ruling Planet: Pluto   **Element:** Water
Lucky Day: Tuesday   **Lucky Numbers:** 2,3,5,8,20,21,41
Colors: Black, Maroon, Brown
Traits: Intense, powerful, steadfast, brave, courageous, devoted, loyal, authentic, complex, jealous, possessive.

SAGITTARIUS
Birthdates: Nov 22 - Dec 21   'The Archer'
Ruling Planet: Jupiter   **Element:** Fire
Lucky Day: Thursday   **Lucky Numbers:** 4,5,9,22,23,45
Colors: Red, Orange, Yellow
Traits: Thoughtful, fun, adventurous, intelligent, generous, dreamers, animal lovers, blunt, rebellious, arrogant, sarcastic.

CAPRICORN
Birthdates: Dec 22 - Jan 19   'The Goat'
Ruling Planet: Saturn   **Element:** Earth
Lucky Day: Saturday   **Lucky Numbers:** 1,7,9,10,16,36,52
Colors: Khaki, Grey, Black, Dark Blue
Traits: Driven, hard worker, persistent, rational, practical, dependable, calculated, cynical, impatient, greedy, unforgiving.

AQUARIUS
Birthdates: Jan 20 - Feb 18   'The Water-Bearer'
Ruling Planet: Uranus   **Element:** Air
Lucky Day: Saturday   **Lucky Numbers:** 2,8,9,11,17,18,35
Colors: Aquamarine, Violet, Turquoise
Traits: Visionary, original, humanitarian, easy going, independent, unpredictable, impersonal, opinionated.

PISCES
Birthdates: Feb 19 - Mar 20   'The Two Fish'
Ruling Planet: Neptune   **Element:** Water
Lucky Day: Thursday   **Lucky Numbers:** 3,5,8,12,14,26
Colors: Lavender, Sea Foam Green, Aquamarine
Traits: Imaginative, intuitive, big-hearted, spiritual, flexible, encouraging, supportive, avoidant, dishonest, gullible, sensitive.

As you can see, the different character traits vary between all the zodiacs; however, the twelve signs can be divided into four groups of three. These four groups are based on the elements, with each zodiac representing an essential type of energy that acts in each of us.

Having this elemental influence through astrology helps us better understand our positive traits, our potential, and focus our energies on positive aspects and guide us through dealing with the negative ones. The four zodiac elements profoundly influence our emotions, behaviors, way of thinking, and fundamental character traits.

EARTH SIGNS
Taurus, Virgo, and Capricorn

These individuals bring us down to earth and are considered 'grounded.' They can be very emotional but mostly conservative and have a realistic view. They tend to be practical, stable, and loyal to their circle of people and stick by them through rough times. However, because they are connected to material reality, they can easily be swayed into a materialistic mindset.

AIR SIGNS
Gemini, Libra, and Aquarius

Zodiac signs under the influence of Air are analytical, intellectual, and rational. The individuals are thinkers, and they tend to be social, friendly, and love to communicate and have relationships with others. Social gatherings, deep philosophical conversations, and good books bring these air signs great love and joy. They enjoy giving their perspective and advice but be careful as they can also be very superficial.

FIRE SIGNS
Aries, Leo, and Sagittarius

If someone has ever inspired you, there is a good chance that they were a Fire sign. These types of individuals are always ready for action, and they are self-aware, intelligent, and creative people. They are physically strong, have a penchant for adventure, and possess a seemingly unlimited supply of immense energy. These people can go from passionate to temperamental quite easily. They are also quick to get angry, but they are just as easy to forgive.

WATER SIGNS
Cancer, Scorpio, and Pisces

Sometimes considered to be as mysterious as the ocean itself, Water signs are highly intuitive, exceptionally emotional, and ultra-sensitive. These individuals tend to have a reasonably close circle, keep to themselves, and rarely do anything openly. Yet, they love deep conversations, intimacy and will always be there to support their loved ones.

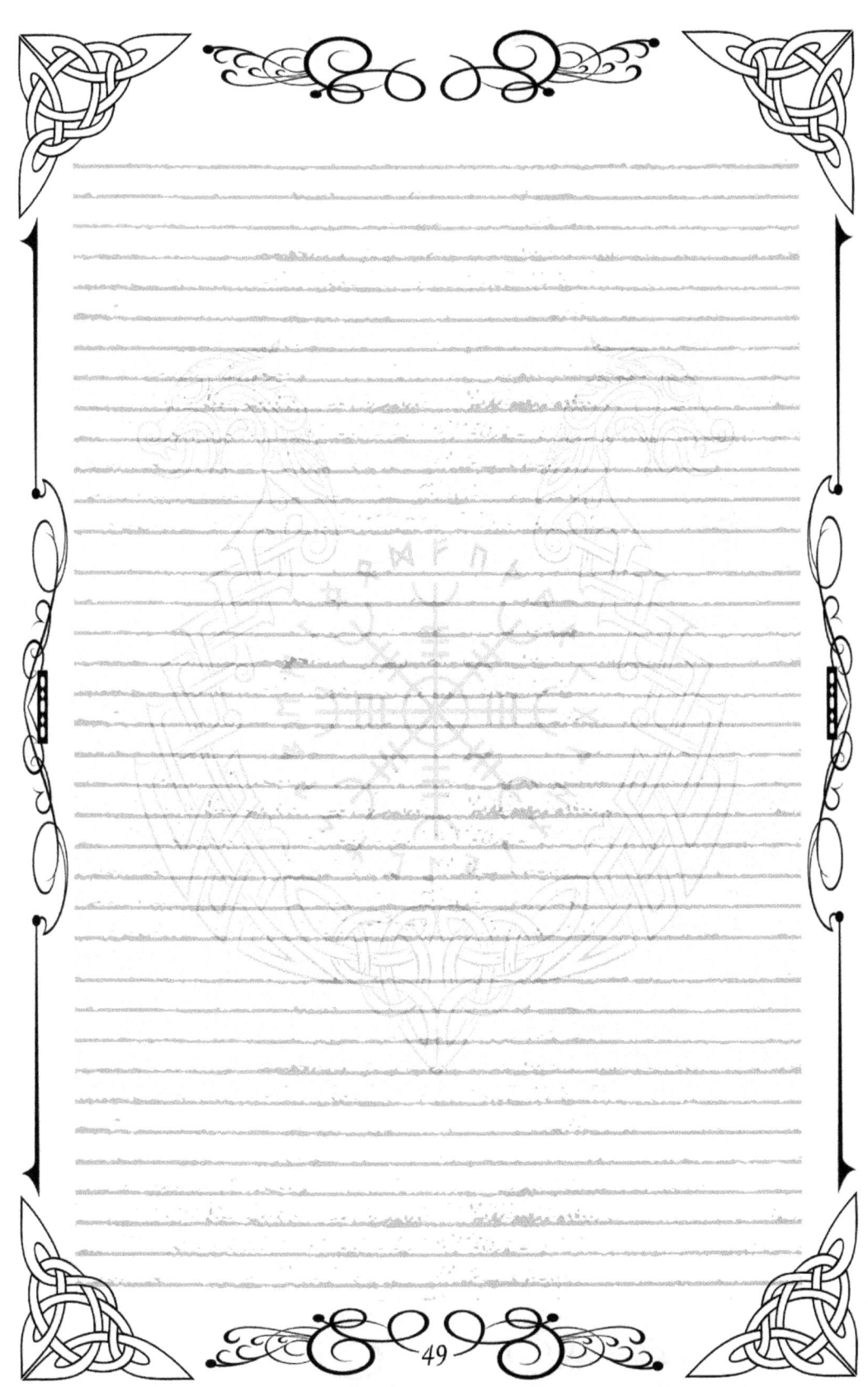

Manifesting with Purpose

A Beginners Guide to Setting Powerful Intentions Using Bindrunes

Setting your Intentions

"You create your thoughts, your thoughts create your intentions, and your intentions create your reality."

Wayne Dyer

Manifesting, or the Law of Attraction, in and of itself is having a strong will and desire to attract a positive change into your life. Your feelings, emotions, and energies are strongly connected to these thoughts of change, which is what sends out vibrations to the universe. In its simplest form, manifesting can be a prayer to a higher power or writing what you want in a journal so you can see it every day.

With bindrunes, we will be discussing how to take those intense feelings, emotions, and energies and attaching them to the runes of your choosing to magnify that power and multiply the vibrations that are sent out to the universe.

When it comes to spellwork and manifesting, the most critical step in determining what you would like to accomplish with your bindrune would be to set your intentions. Think of it as the kick-starting spark with your creative power that accelerates your desires outward to be heard by the universe so the Law of Attraction can start working its magick.

You may have heard the phrase "intention is everything," which is mostly correct, but it goes much deeper than just having the intent to manifest something.

Thinking of your intentions requires you to sit down, think, and write out what you want to accomplish. We need to think about every step along the way and not just the end result. Therefore, setting your intention will involve thinking about getting to that desired result, what you need to do, and potentially what you need help with to accomplish this goal.

Following is a list of steps that can help you set powerful intentions. Start at the beginning and work your way through the steps. I recommend that you have a journal or blank sheet of paper to record all your thoughts and ideas throughout this process.

CREATE A PERSONAL RITUAL

Depending on what you know about rituals, this can be as elaborate or simple as you want it to be. If you feel the need to cast a circle with salt, call the deities and ground yourself, then go for it. This could also include a simple meditation to clear your mind so you can plan your thoughts in an optimal soulful state.

Your ritual should be unique to you and how you love to do things. Sometimes, all it takes is to make your favorite drink (which could be tea, coffee, water, a glass of wine, etc.), sit with your journal under the stars, and write down your intentions.

Whatever your ritual looks like, make sure it gives you joy and leaves you feeling uplifted and full of inspiration. Then, give yourself some space away from any distractions and at least half an hour of uninterrupted time. This is your time to focus and 'unplug' from the world by turning off your devices and letting your friends and loved ones know that you have plans.

Take this time to relax, breathe deeply, clear your mind, listen to the sounds around you (especially if you are outside within nature), hear what the universe is whispering, and feel every part of your body unwind as you let go of all your worries.

ALLOW YOURSELF TO MEDITATE

Meditation is an excellent way for us to clear our minds of any thoughts, breathe deeply, and become attuned to the universal energies around us. There are many different ways in which you can meditate, so I encourage you to find a practice that works best for you.

The easiest way to achieve a meditative state is to focus on your breath. Sit or lay in a comfortable position, close your eyes, clear your mind of any thoughts, and with each breath, imagine that you are inhaling a pure cleansing white light through your nostrils, and exhaling all your doubt and worries through your mouth.

Continue to fully relax your body as you focus on breathing in and out. If you have trouble letting go of all the thoughts racing through your mind, you can put on some soft music to help you. There are also some great meditation apps out there to help you focus better if you need to utilize them.

Once you feel relaxed, calm, and peaceful, you can open your eyes and start the writing process.

If you are unsure or don't know, in the next step, we will go over the specifics of what to write.

BE SPECIFIC AND GET CREATIVE

Start to write down what your heart truly desires. Go crazy if you want. Dream big because this is your life, and there are no rules. Let go of all societal clichés and taboos and just let your imagination run wild.

This is your chance to get creative and dare to dream up the most amazing experiences you can think of. Extend your consciousness into allowing yourself to think about new adventures that you would enjoy and love to experience.

As you are jotting down your thoughts, it is paramount to remember and be mindful of how each of these ideas makes you feel. How you feel about each of these desires is the actual spark to initiating your manifesting work. Feeling is everything. If you do not feel good about a particular thought or intention, this may not be the right path.

We will do a small exercise on the power of your feelings associated with your thoughts and desires. What do you think would be the top three desires people would like to manifest into their lives? If you said money, you are correct. However, love and fame are also high on the list of typical desires.

We will use money as an example. I want you to close your eyes and think about how your life would be if you had the financial freedom to do whatever you want and go wherever you please. What would this mean for you or your family? Think about all the aspects of your life that extra money could influence.

Dig deep into your subconscious mind, imagine living in your dream house, driving your dream car, or traveling to your dream destinations. Now I want you to visualize and see in your minds-eye that this is all TRUE. You live in your dream house. You drive your dream car. You travel to your favorite places.

How does that make you feel?

Are you experiencing a sense of freedom? Maybe you have an enormous amount of relief associated with acquiring these things. Do you feel empowered? Loved? Courageous? Brave? Euphoric? Catharsis?

Now pause for a moment and sit with these feelings. Feel the warmth in your belly and the pure light of happiness shining from inside you? The power that is emanating from this feel-good awareness is intoxicating, isn't it?

Those internal reactions and perceptions make your desires seen and heard by the universe when you manifest. When you start to feel what you want, you begin a sacred creation process with the mighty universe. When your feelings are connected to your thoughts and desires, the universe listens and responds.

Apart from the immense feelings associated with your desires, you will also have to be concise, clear, and specific when writing down your intentions. The universe thrives on specificity and detailed requests. So, dig deep into the details of what you are trying to manifest. What kind of things, people, places, or experiences are linked to that desire?

A good practice to maintain when writing your intentions and desires on your worksheet is to divide the page into two columns. You will write down all your thoughts, desires, activities, or experiences you wish to manifest into your life on the left-hand side.

On the right-hand side, you will write down all the feelings associated with those thoughts, desires, activities, and experiences. As you are writing, you need to try and feel that what you want to manifest has already happened or come true and record its associated feelings.

I have provided an example worksheet for guidance while you are working with the intention-setting process. Feel free to use the chart to record your intentions or use it as a template to create your workbook or journal to keep all your thoughts in a safe place.

THOUGHTS/DESIRES	FEELINGS

THOUGHTS/DESIRES	FEELINGS

PRIORITIZE YOUR INTENTIONS

Once you have a list of your desired intentions, the next step is to go through and prioritize them according to what you feel is most important to you in the present moment. On a scale of 1 to 10 (1 is 'I need it now,' and 10 is 'it can wait'), go through your worksheet and number the desires you have listed.

If you enjoy living an organized life full of schedules and plans, you may also put specific dates beside each one of your desires to set a deadline for yourself. This is also an enjoyable and exciting activity to do when you look back in a year or two to see the progress of your manifesting journey over time.

Keep this list on hand, as we will need to refer to it in the next chapter: Choosing Runes to Match your Intent.

TAKING ACTION

When you have completed listing your desires in priority of importance, you can now go back and make a list of actions you can start to take for each one to get the ball rolling.

There is no need to overcomplicate this process. Simply write down one thing that you can take action on within the next week to help guide the universe in the right direction. Making a list of activities will help set a clear path in your subconscious mind for things to start manifesting.

The universe will always respond to inspired action, and this could be something as simple as putting $5 aside for your dream home. The very 'act' of putting that $5 aside lets the universe know that you are strongly connected to this desire. You already feel that this has become

a reality for you. In turn, it creates a more powerful vibration that the universe will listen and respond to.

No matter which way you look at it, there needs to be some action to start manifesting. If manifesting was as easy as thinking about something that would materialize in our reality, then most of the population would be rich because we would all win the lottery just by thinking we won the lottery.

If it were that easy to create our realities, we would all be living in mansions and driving sports cars. The universe works in mysterious ways, and we have known this for a long time. There are parts of the vast expanse of space that we as a human species are yet to understand, but we have come to one conclusion; we know that there is an enormous amount of energy in all corners of the universe.

We need to tap into this energy because all living things are made up of this energy, and we all have it within us. We need to find that cosmic connection by taking action and aligning our energies with the universe.

TRUST AND SURRENDER

Now that you have listed your thoughts and desires, prioritized them, and took action to start the manifesting process, the time has come for you to let them go. I know that this may sound a little redundant because we have just spent so much time setting our intentions, but this is a necessary step to allow your intentions to incubate in the etheric realm.

For some, this can be the hardest part of the process, but we need to do this so we prevent ourselves from placing obstacles in the way

that might prevent the manifestation from happening. Distraction can be a powerful helper to unblock some of these vibrational obstacles.

When you let your intentions go, you do not have to forget about them altogether. Instead, you will need to hold on to what the feelings were when you created your list. Then, hold the essence of those feelings in your heart as you move forward with your life, and trust that the universe has a divine plan of action for you.

If we cannot surrender our intentions to the universe, we may experience too much energetic resistance. Unfortunately, many people tend to obsess about their intentions, place themselves under pressure to make something happen to move it along, or watch like a hawk to see if there are any signs to prove that the universe has responded.

This would be a good way for your intentions to get lost in the non-physical realm because the vibrations get 'stage fright' and will not release outward. Instead, we need to trust that the universe heard your request, and by surrendering our intentions, we can start making these desires unfold in the best way possible to nurture your soul.

Take your journal or worksheet and put it away for a while. Feel free to embellish a pretty envelope to store your intentions in a safe spot or place your journal among the other books on a bookshelf.

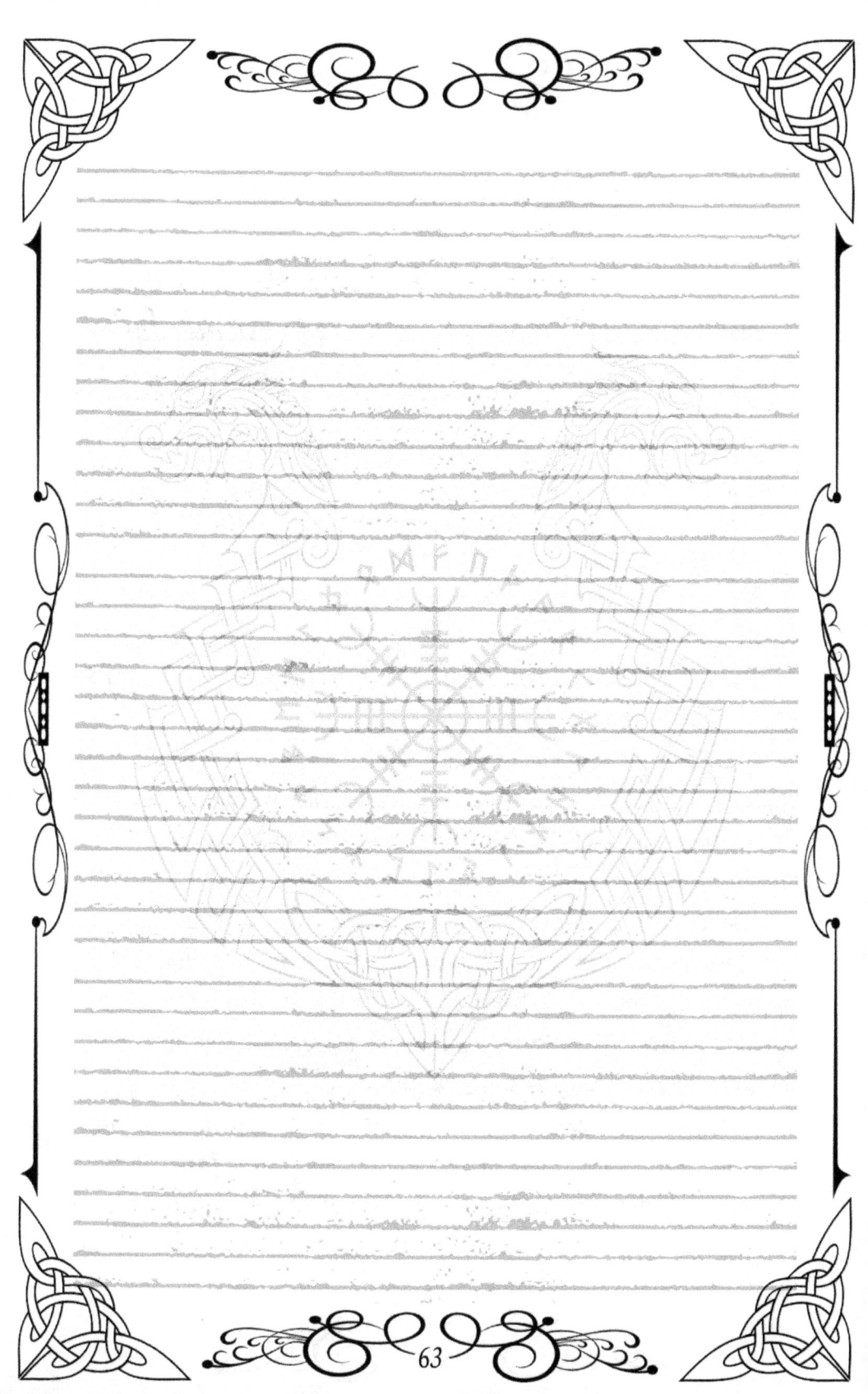

CREATING A GRATITUDE LOOP

"Gratitude is the healthiest of all human emotions. The more you express gratitude for what you have, the more likely you will have even more to express gratitude for."

Zig Ziglar

Being grateful for this present moment can send out a massive shift in your vibrational energy. The feeling of gratefulness comes from your thoughts and feelings, and your emotions connected to each are being emitted out into the universe.

Gratitude, joy, love, and appreciation are among a select few emotions that emit the highest energy frequencies. When we attune our lives to these emotions and feelings, we are closer to achieving alignment with our desires.

Living a life of thankfulness every day will create a gratitude loop. This loop happens when we become immersed in the unlimited cycle of abundant energy. When we are grateful for what we already have and possess, the universe will respond by rewarding us with more things to appreciate and be thankful for.

If we surround ourselves in a constant state of gratitude, we will find that our intentions and desires will be manifesting faster than ever before. Feeling gratitude every day will attract more reasons to feel grateful.

This cycle will continue throughout your manifesting journey. You feel grateful, the universe sends you the things you desire, and therefore you feel even more grateful. In turn, receiving these blessings will emit even more gratitude to the universe, and again, brings you more experiences or desires that you can be grateful for.

You will have to do a few things first to start your shift into a gratitude loop. However, this should only take you approximately 5 - 10 minutes to complete.

First, start to visualize about 5 - 10 things you already have in your life (not what you desire or wish to manifest) you are thankful for. Then, write these down on a piece of paper or in your journal, leaving space for additional information.

Second, I want you to focus and channel your emotions into those blessings you have in your life. How does it **feel** to have these things in your current reality? This should be making you feel good about the people, places, and things you have in your life. After a few minutes of feeling good, write down those feelings next to the appropriate item in your list.

Here are a couple of examples from my list:

"I am grateful to have a roof over my head, a warm bed to sleep in, and clean water to drink."

"I am thankful and appreciative for the support I receive from my friends and family."

Sometimes we find it hard to think of what we are most thankful for because we don't even notice something that we utilize in our everyday lives and most likely take it for granted.

To keep your gratitude loop active and going, it is important to read from your list every day. It should not be seen as a one-time task because we need to emit our feelings of thankfulness every day to keep our vibrations raised.

If you find that you have more to add to your list, feel free to make your list longer. Do not hold back. The more you give to the universe, the more you will receive.

If you need some assistance with thinking outside the box for different things to be grateful for, you can always check out the 'Attitude of Gratitude' journal by J.C. Marco on Amazon. This journal features a 30-Day Challenge to help you start your gratitude loop, and assist with building your practice of daily gratefulness.

> "What you think you become.
> What you feel you attract.
> What you imagine you create."
>
> Buddha

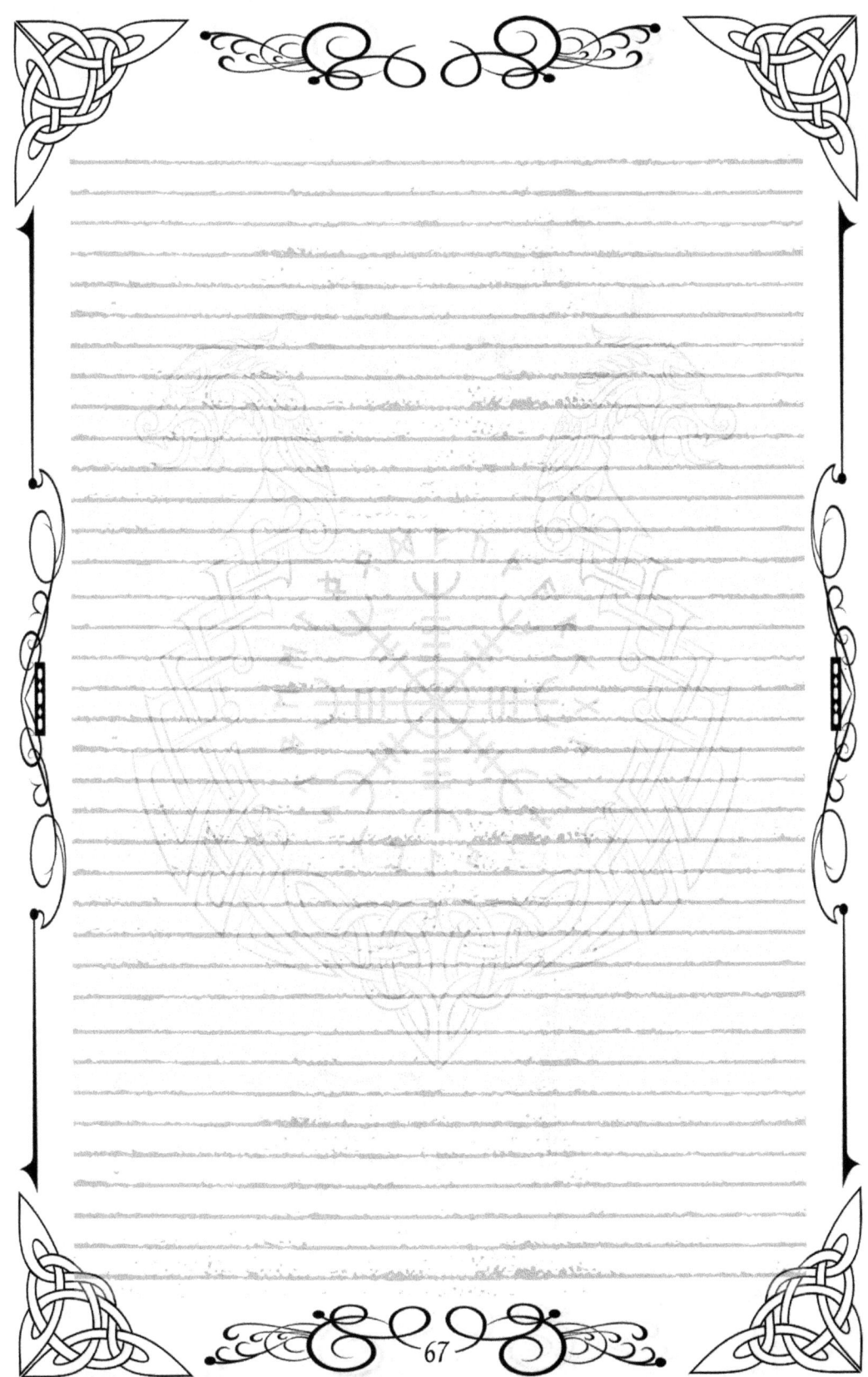

Choosing Runes to match your Intent

Your intentions are deeply rooted in your emotions and feelings, and you can easily find multiple runes that represent these emotions. Whether you are a beginner in creating bindrunes or an advanced rune caster, it is best to keep it simple and avoid over-complicating things.

Looking back at the list you created when writing down your intentions, we will need to focus on your feelings associated with your desires.

It is time to start assigning specific runes to each of the feelings attached to your intentions. This can prove difficult, as some runes have multiple or ambiguous meanings, so take your time and do not rush through this crucial step.

Go through the list of runes (pages 29-32) and read about each one and its meanings. Then, next to each of your feelings, jot down which runes best fit the purpose of your intention or most closely represent the feeling.

Some of the runes will be obvious choices as to whether they will serve your purpose or not, but it is still necessary to go through each one so you can consider all the possibilities.

Once you have chosen the runes that closely match or compliment your intentions, it is time to narrow down the choices so that you only have a maximum of three or four depending on the bindrune design you intend to create.

THREE CIRCLE METHOD

If you believe in destiny, fate, divine intervention, and that 'things happen for a reason,' the Three Circle Method might be what you need for the universe to decide which runes you will be using. This method does require that you have a physical set of runes available. If you do not have a set of runes, there are many different images that you can find online. Search for a picture of the runes that speak to you, print them and cut them out to separate all the runes. Once you have all your runes together, set them to the side.

The three circles that I will show you are also a different approach to rune casting. This arrangement can be used to do quick readings if you have any questions that you need answers to, but we will be using this method to help us decide which runes we will be using to create our bindrune. The first thing you want to do is draw three circles on a piece of paper or cloth and arrange them like this:

When you look at this diagram, you will notice an inner circle, a middle ring, and an outer ring. Each of these three sections will be associated with different facets of your life or personality.

The easiest and most common way to categorize the three sections, from inner to outer, would be past, present, and future. However, if you would like to have a more detailed 'casting' based on personal aspects, then the inner circle would represent 'self,' the middle ring would represent your 'influences,' and the outer ring would represent 'future events.'

Whichever way you choose to classify each circle is up to you. Do what feels right.

With the circles drawn out on paper or cloth, you will now 'cast' or 'throw' the runes onto the diagram to see where they will land. The positions they land in will give you the interpretations for each circle and how you decided to associate them.

Typically, only six runes are used, but feel free to cast as many as you think will be necessary. If you have your own set of runes, they are most likely already contained in a cloth bag of some sort. If you printed out the runes and cut them apart, place the runes in a bowl or bag so you can quickly draw from the pack to select the runes you will be using.

Gently shake the bag or bowl of runes, and while doing so, think about what it is you desire. You can also think about a question that you would like answered. Then, while keeping the desire or question in your mind, choose six runes from the bag or bowl and drop them onto the three circles.

Notice where the runes land? The locations will offer you the guidance needed to answer any questions you may have and help you with your manifesting goals. Keep track of each position and write them down so you can refer to it later.

Generally, you would like to see at least one rune in each circle, but if there are two or more, then write them all down, and you can decide which one to use after reading their interpretations.

Once you have at least one rune for each circle, you can now go back to see what each one means (pages 29-32) to get a better understanding of the message you are receiving from the universe.

As you are reading the definitions, refer back to your intention worksheet. Are the interpretations closely aligning with any of the intentions that you listed? Are the meanings similar to the feelings that you have associated with your desires?

If the meanings of the runes are closely comparable to what you have written down, then it looks like the universe has provided you the runes to use in your bindrune.

Do not worry if the interpretations are not closely related to your desires and intentions; this may be the universe trying to give you a different message. On the other hand, if you are happy with the meanings, feel free to use those in your bindrune.

> "Everything you want is out there waiting for you to ask. Everything you want also wants you. But you have to take action to get it."
> - Jack Canfield

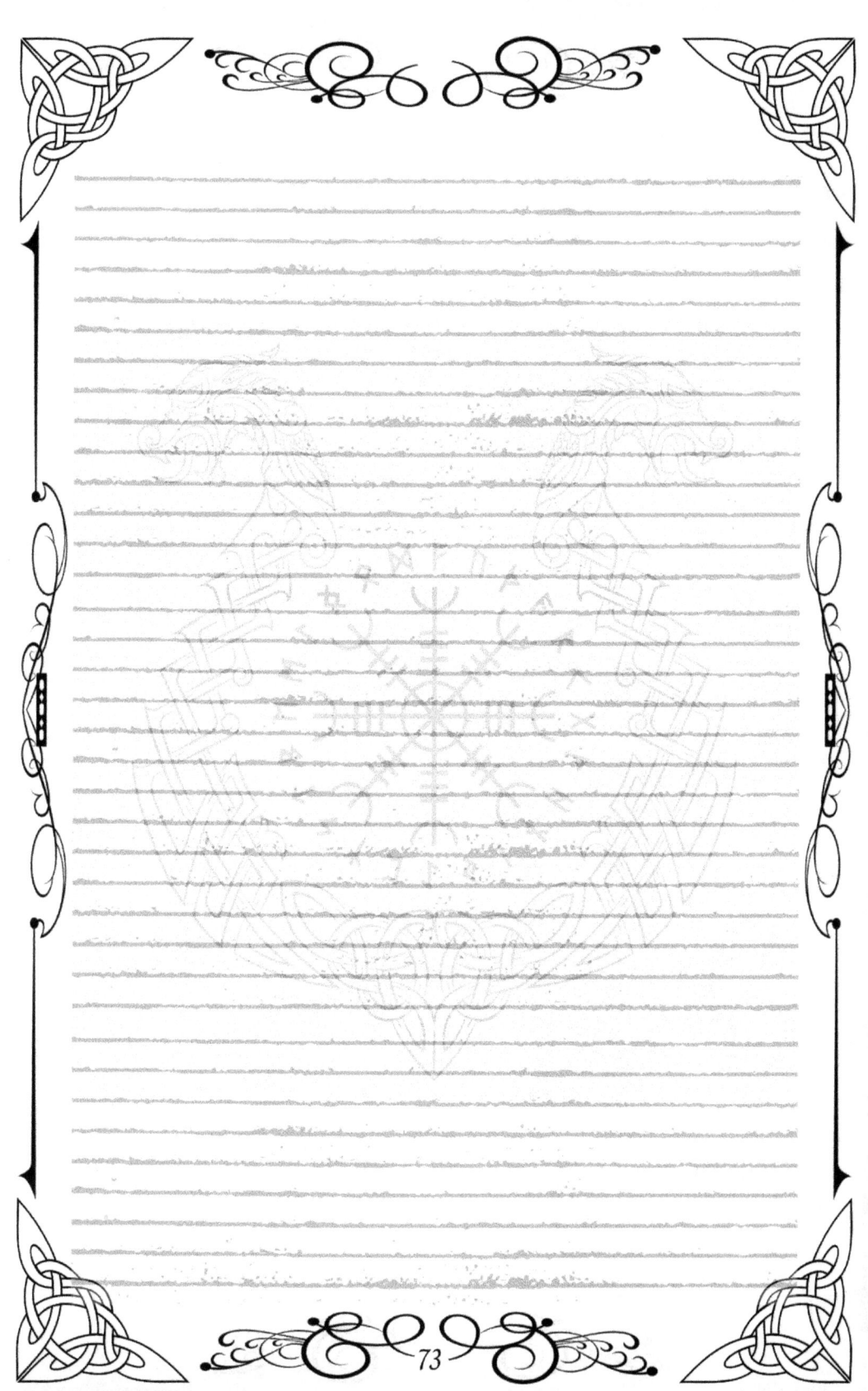

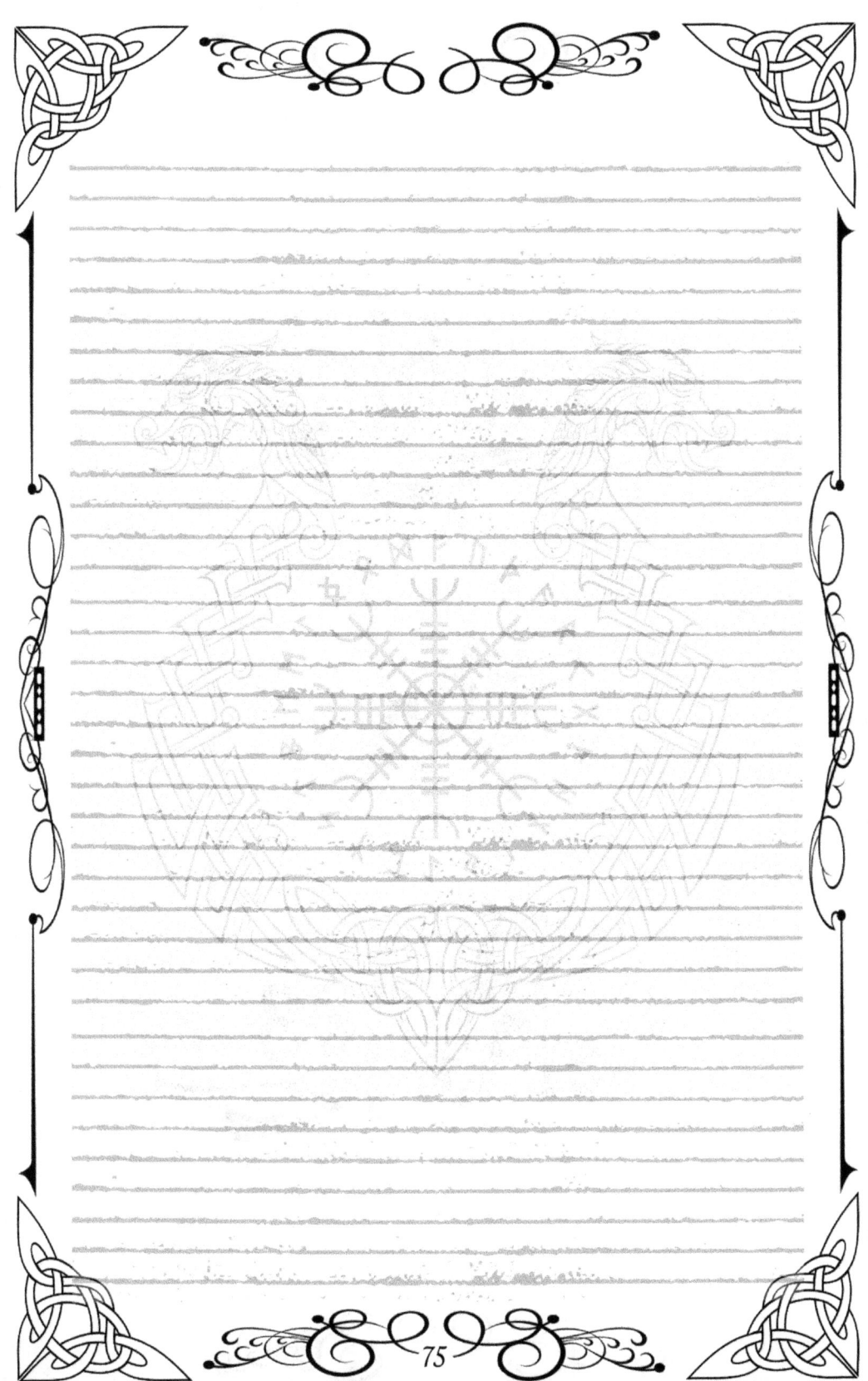

Combining the Runes

When the time comes to combine the runes, this is the fun and creative stage. Once you have carefully selected your runes, or if you preferred to have the fates decide which runes you will be using, it is time to start the creative process of combining them.

You should feel calm, relaxed, and at peace during this stage as you draw out different variations of your bindrune design. If it helps, feel free to put on some relaxing music or a nature soundtrack to get you into a peaceful state of relaxation.

This process should be enjoyable for you, so take as much time as you need. Open your mind, clear your thoughts, and just let your creativity flow through you and onto the paper.

Once you start creating your bindrune, you will be inspired to try different layouts and combinations. Try to draw as many designs as you can until you find one that speaks to you and embodies the feelings and desires you wish to manifest.

As you create your bindrune, it is vital to be mindful of any 'hidden' runes that you may inadvertently create within the design.

Along with any hidden runes, you may also want to look for any 'reversed' runes, as these could negatively impact the energy you are trying to achieve when making your bindrune.

Depending on the style of bindrune you wish to create, some types have little to no reversed or hidden runes, and other kinds will contain many hidden and reversed runes. If you are a beginner, I would suggest a more uncomplicated style, such as a same-stave or radial bindrune.

It may take some time to identify all the hidden or reversed runes in your design, what they mean, and how they will impact your intentions. However, it is good to know what you are working with because these extra runes can change the energy drastically.

In the following two chapters, we will go over how to identify the hidden runes and any reversed rune meanings. Be mindful and consider adding zodiac or elemental signs to strengthen your bindrune energy (pages 35-46).

One of the easiest tricks I found when creating my bindrune is to draw them out on graph paper. The squares that it provides serve as an excellent marker to center your runes and layer them together. Please use the following few pages as a creative space to start the process.

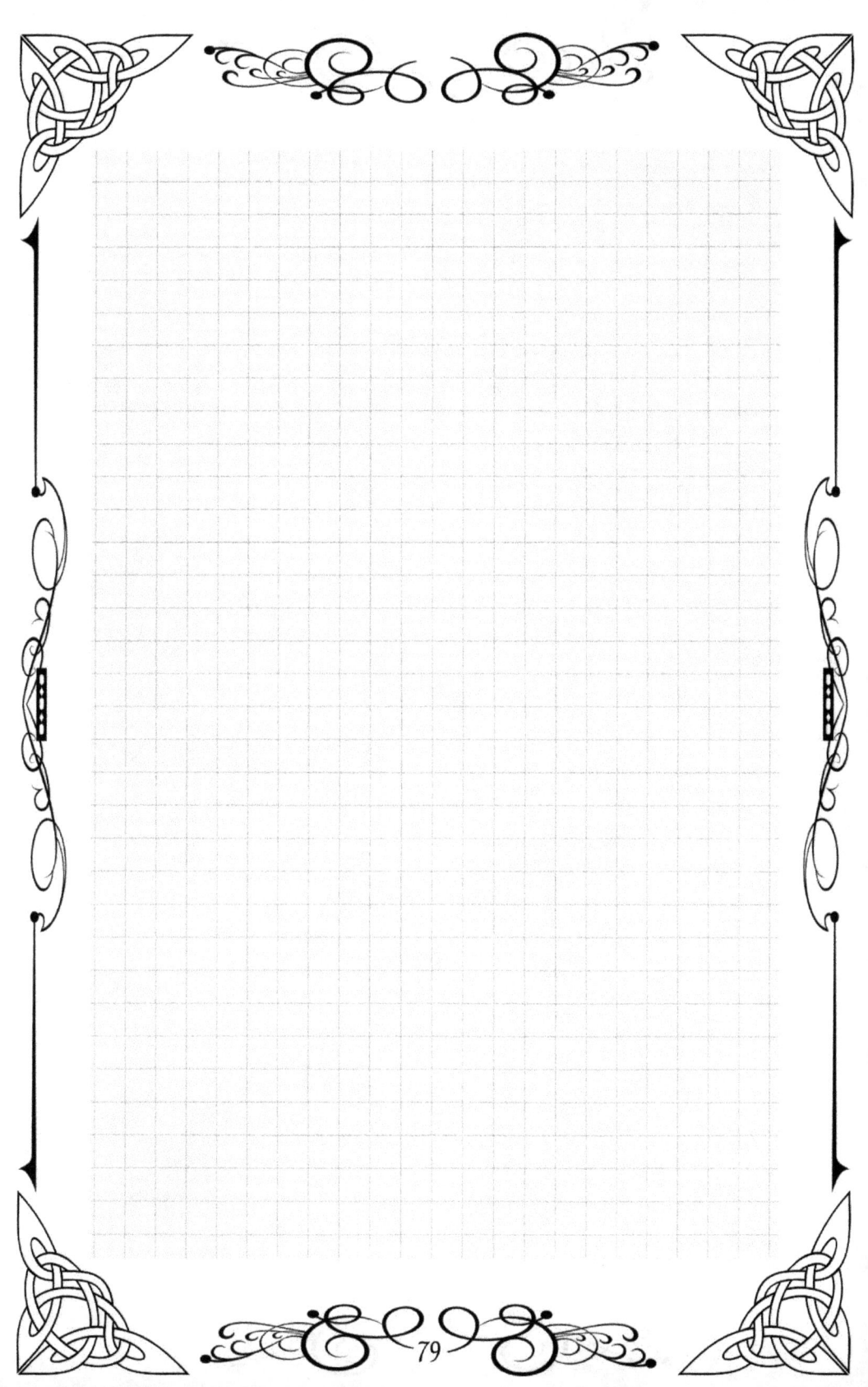

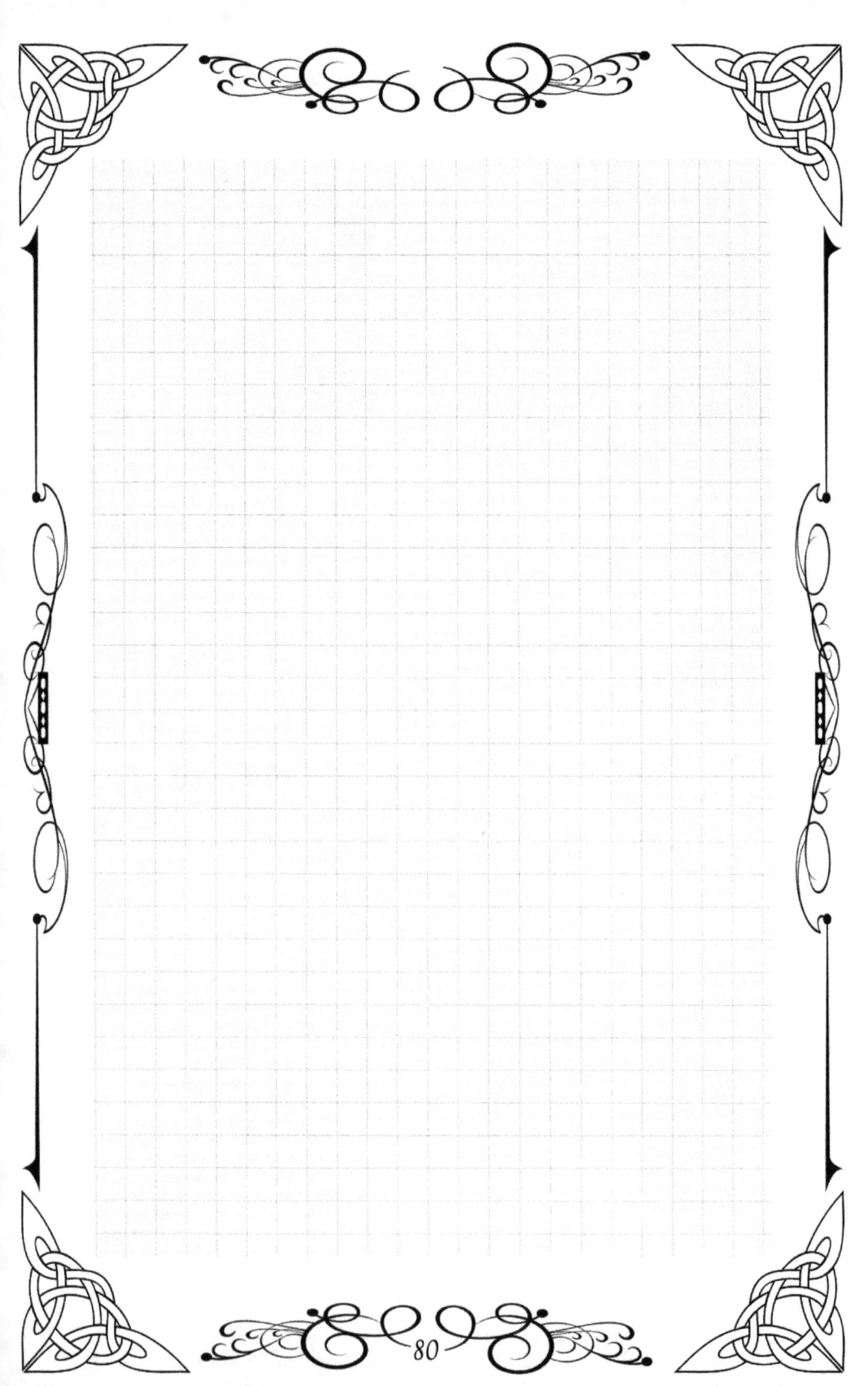

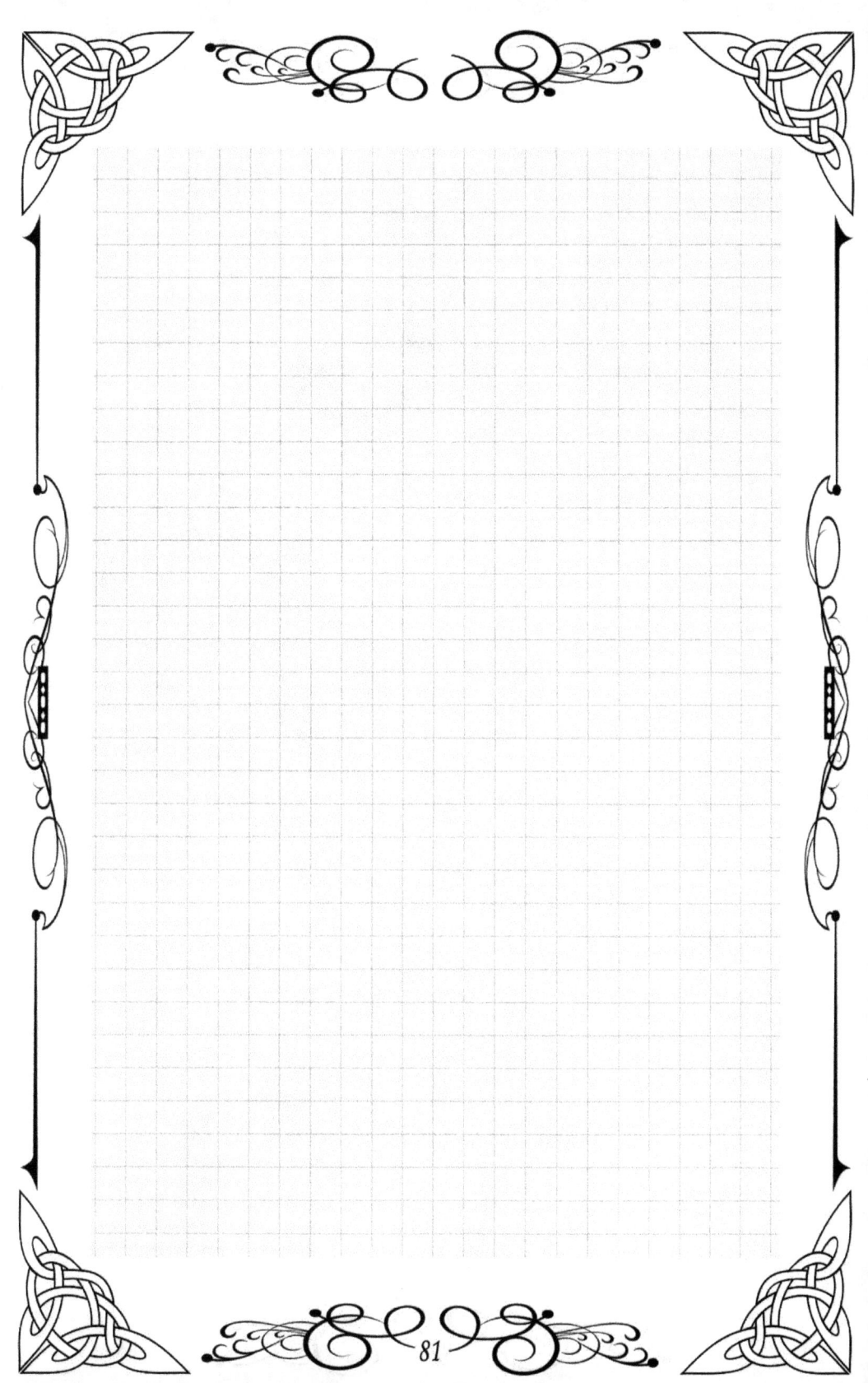

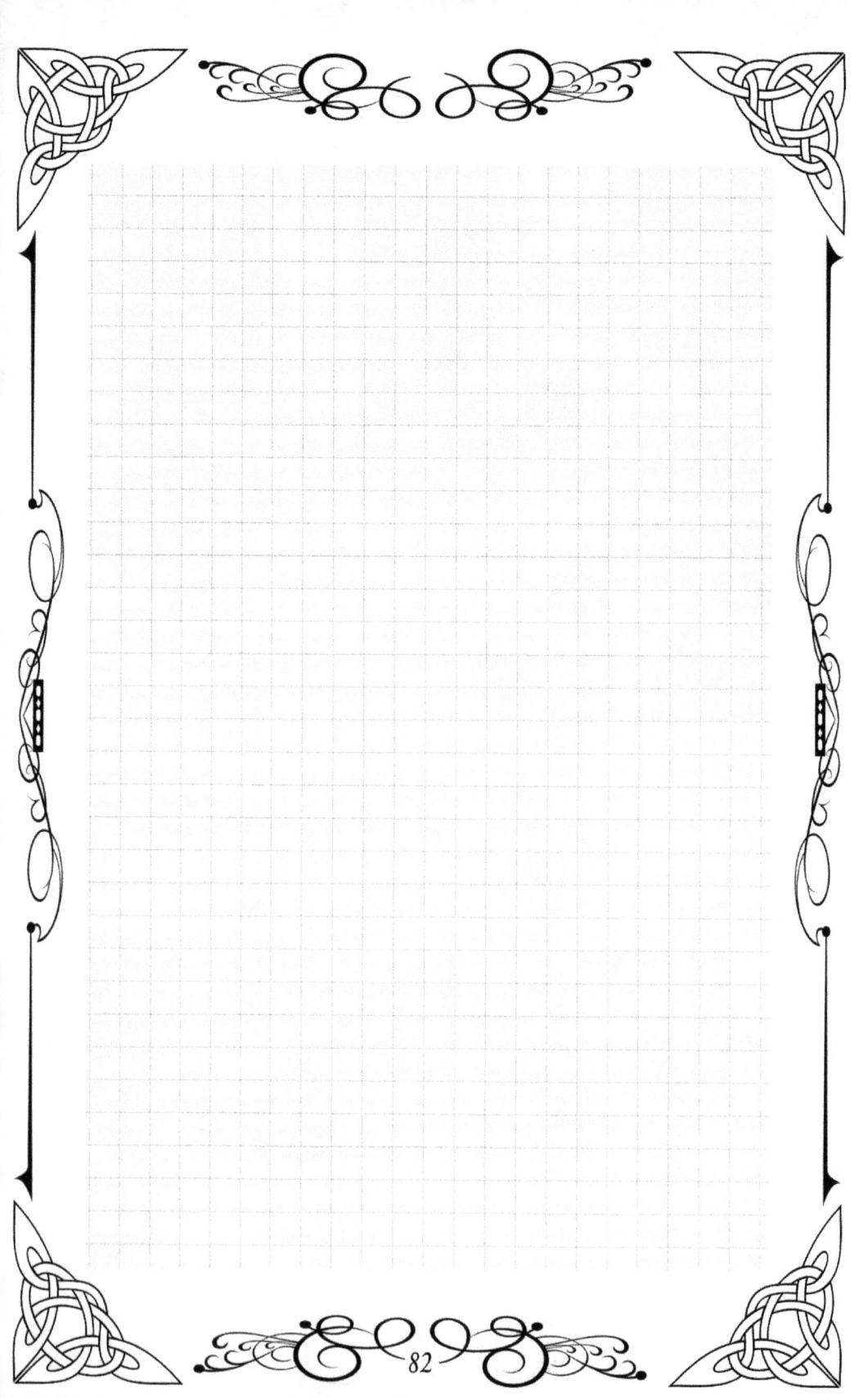

Looking for Hidden Runes

 When you are creating your bindrunes, there is a good possibility that you will also be adding additional runes that you did not originally intend to have without even knowing it. We need to keep an eye out for these 'hidden runes,' as they may inadvertently change the energies and direction of your manifesting goals.

 Having 'extra' runes show up in your design is not necessarily bad, as this is part of the creative process. However, even though they may not have been in your original choices, we need to know what these 'hidden' runes mean for our bindrune energy.

 However, there is one specific rune that we need to be mindful of that is easily missed. The rune Isa, which is literally just a vertical line, is technically going to be 'hidden' in every single bindrune you do. Furthermore, if you look at all the runes individually, how many single runes have a vertical line already in their design?

 Isa will be everywhere you look now that I have pointed it out, so knowing what it means will ultimately help you decipher what your bindrune energies will look like when it is completed.

 Sometimes it is a pleasant surprise to find hidden runes in your design. Maybe you were on the fence about certain ones, decided not to use them, and later seen them reappear within your bindrune. This is a delightful gift from the universe, letting you know that you are on the right path, the runes may have something to tell you, or they have a personal connection to you and your goals.

 Do you remember the four examples of freeform bindrunes that I created earlier? To refresh your memory, these are the three runes that I have chosen to bind together:

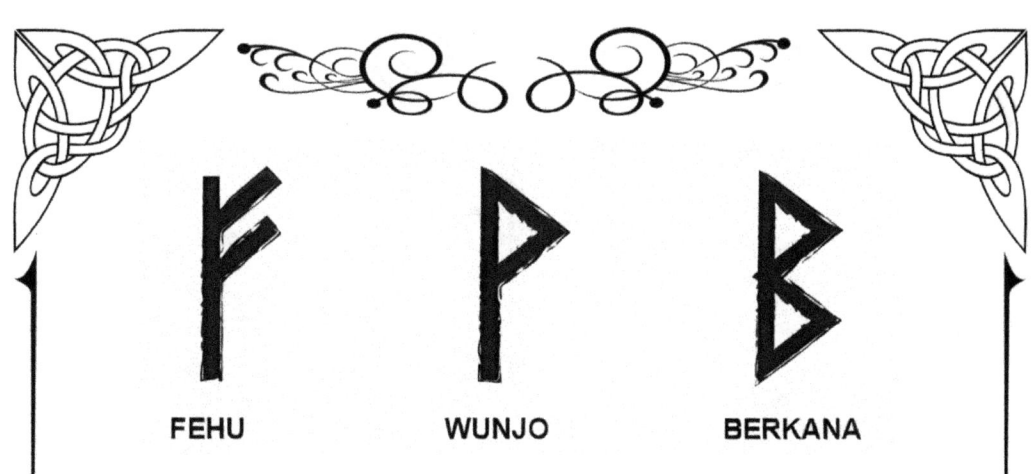

| FEHU | WUNJO | BERKANA |

Now, take a look at a refined drawing of example 2 from earlier:

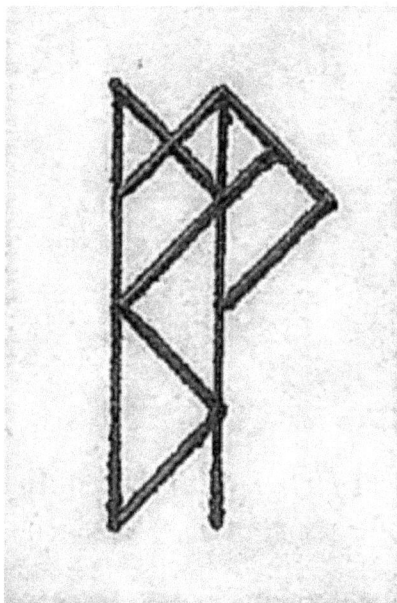

In this example bindrune that I have created, the two vertical lines are Berkana and Wunjo, respectively. Can you see Berkana on the left and Wunjo on the right? Fehu is directly placed on top of Berkana, with their vertical lines identically overlapping. Can you see all three runes independently?

If we look back to the previous chapter (Getting to Know the Runes) listing all the runic symbols, how many additional 'hidden' runes can you see in this bindrune example?

I want to test your knowledge and see how well you studied the runes. In the example bindrune that I have drawn for you, not including the original three runes that I have used, you should be able to find and name thirteen additional 'hidden' runes. Grab a pen or pencil and see if you can find them all.

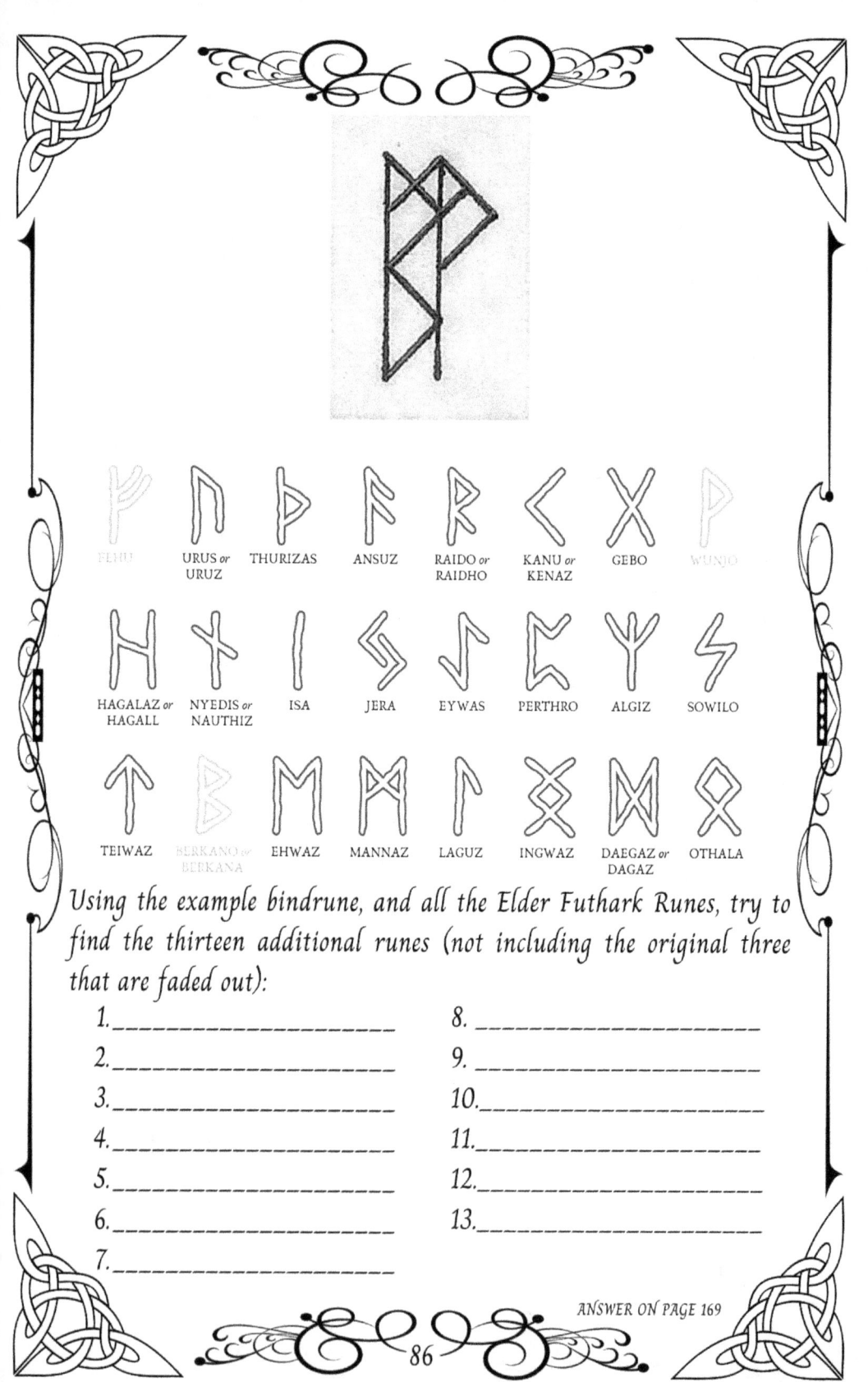

Using the example bindrune, and all the Elder Futhark Runes, try to find the thirteen additional runes (not including the original three that are faded out):

1. _____
2. _____
3. _____
4. _____
5. _____
6. _____
7. _____
8. _____
9. _____
10. _____
11. _____
12. _____
13. _____

ANSWER ON PAGE 169

As you can see, it is effortless to start with a simple design and suddenly create a bindrune that is way more complex than you may have originally intended. My example has grown from a simple three rune design to a more complex bindrune with sixteen individual runes and sixteen individual meanings linked to it.

If you are a beginner, it may be easier to choose a more straightforward design to start with, such as a same-stave or radial bindrune. These two styles will limit the number of hidden runes you will find and save you lots of time from starting over to remove them.

With your favorite design(s) that you have created, use the next page to determine what hidden runes you have within your creation.

What hidden runes can you find in each design? Make a list under each one and use the next page if you need more room to write.

Draw your favorite designs on the next couple of pages (your top two or three choices):

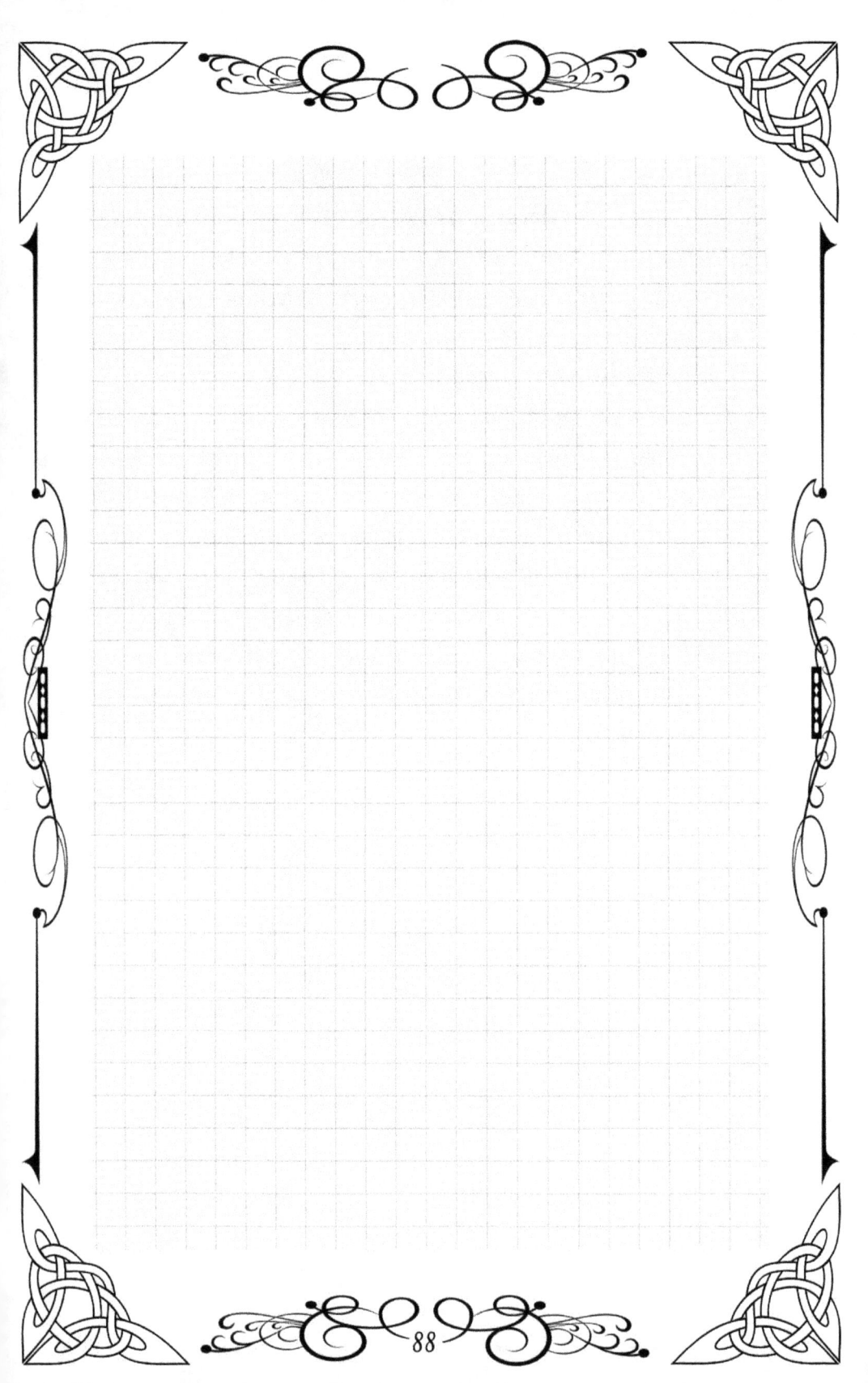

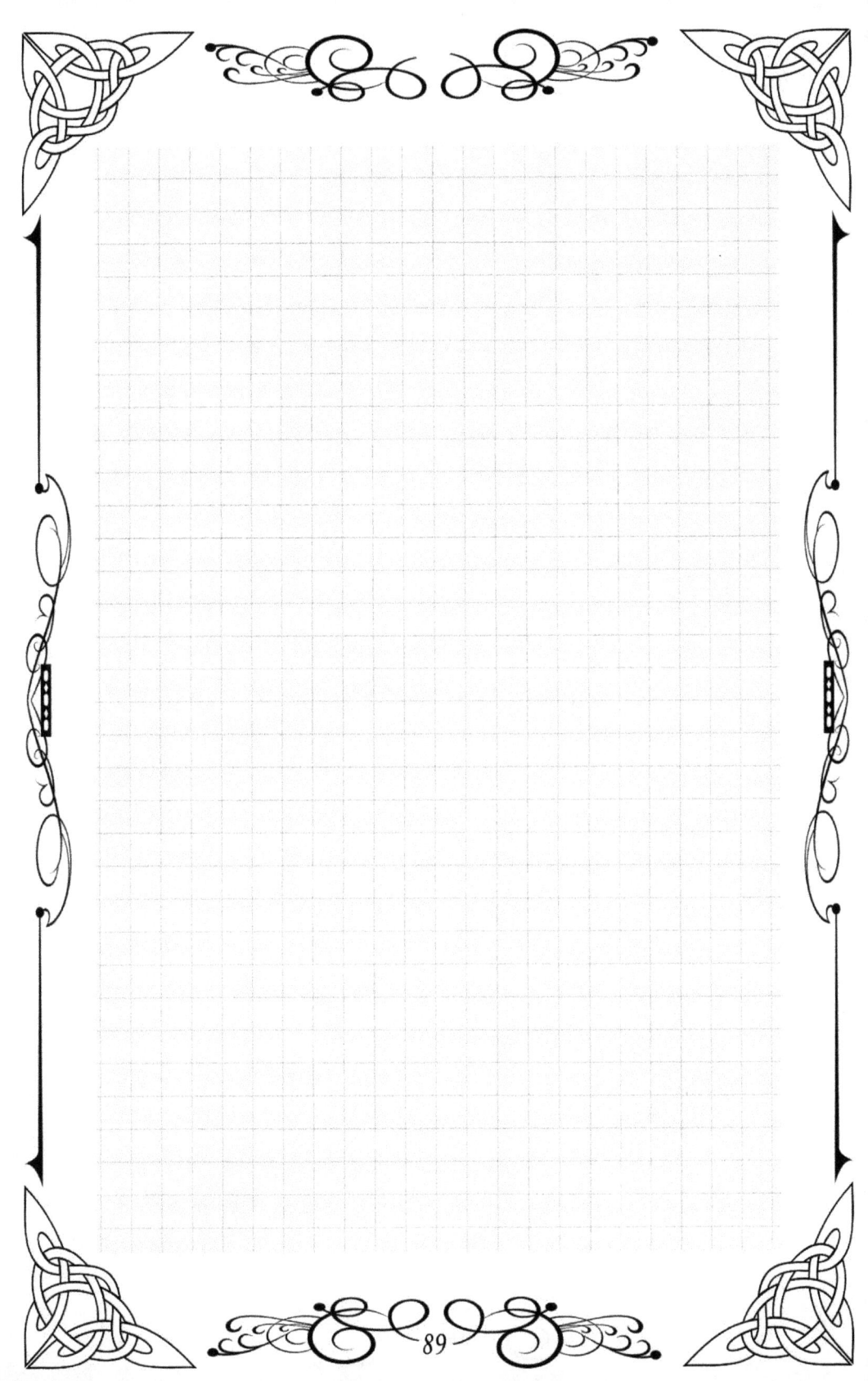

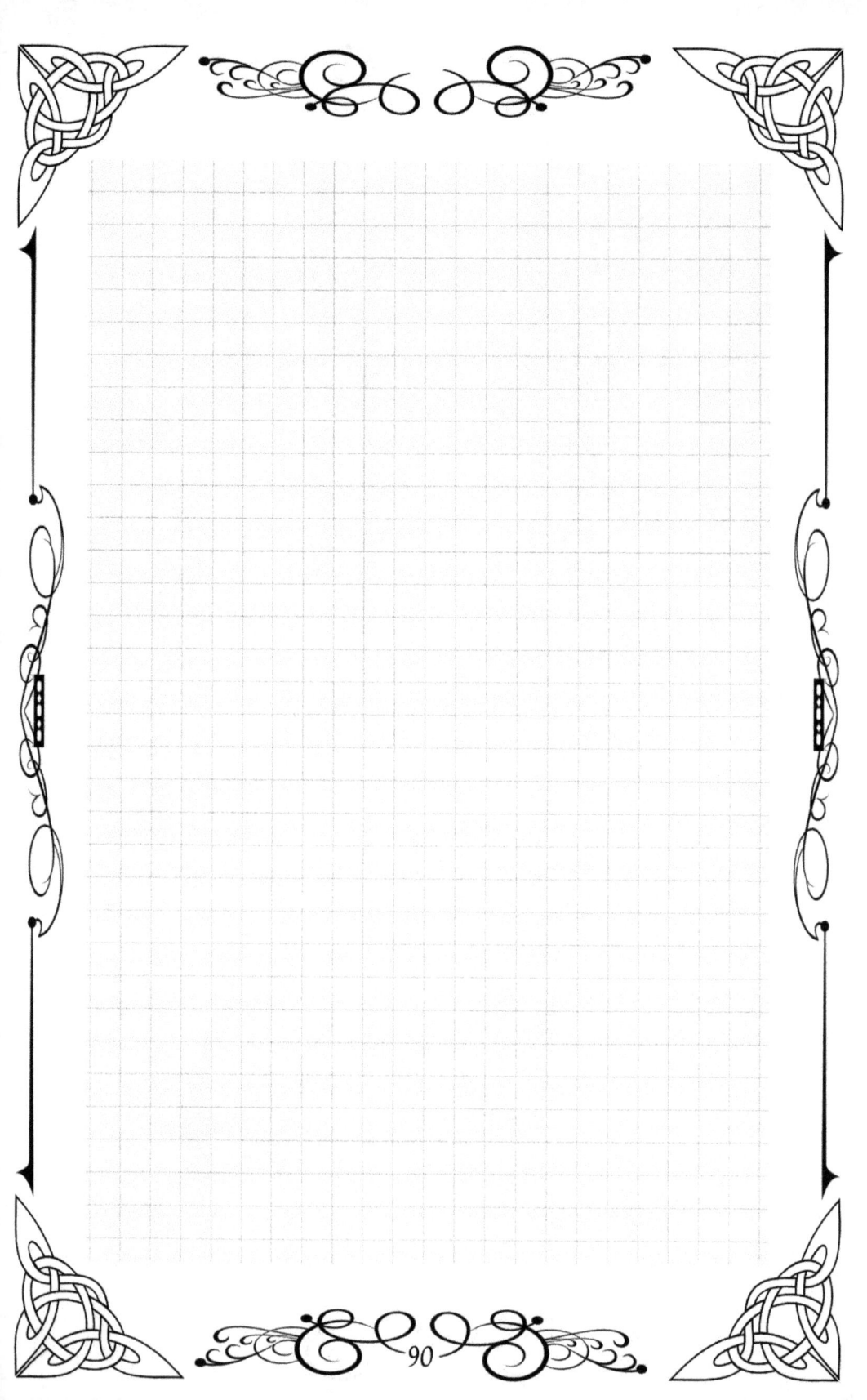

Looking for Reversed Runes

If you are knowledgeable about the runes and complete frequent castings or readings, you will know that some runes also have reversed or negative meanings. Some people tend to think of all the runes as having one translation, but if you are part of the select few who want to create intense energy in your bindrune, knowing the reversed meanings will be extremely helpful. This will also help you to pinpoint if there will be any negativity that you wish to eliminate from your design.

If you are new to learning about the Elder Futhark, I am referring to runes with a different shape or structure when they are turned upside down. Rune users who cast readings for themselves or others would pick runes from a velvet bag, and the way they were drawn (either right side up or upside down) is what the universal message would convey.

Nine runes do not have a mirror image, meaning they are the same whether they are right side up or turned upside down. It would be beneficial to consider one of these nine as a base or center for your bindrune as there would not be any negative connotations attached to it.

If you were to turn this book upside down and look at the nine runes above, you would notice that they are the same no matter how you look at them. This means that they do not have a negative or 'reversed' meaning.

Next, we will go over the remaining fifteen runes to see their meanings when they are reversed or upside down.

	UPRIGHT		REVERSED

FEHU "fay-hoo"
Reversed or Negative Meaning:
Struggles, low confidence, loss of personal property or income, greed, burnout, discord, low self-esteem.

URUZ "oo-rooze"
Reversed or Negative Meaning:
Loss of stamina, health, or ability, misdirected causes, barriers, weakness, obsession, inconsistency.

THURIZAS "thur-ee-saws"
Reversed or Negative Meaning:
Betrayal, defenselessness, obsession, resentment, animosity, danger, compulsion, hatred, vulnerability.

ANSUZ "awn-sooz"
Reversed or Negative Meaning:
Miscommunication, manipulation, dishonesty, confusion, misconception, deceit, misunderstanding.

RAIDHO "rye-though"
Reversed or Negative Meaning:
Disruption, harshness, discrimination, being unreasonable, irrational, rigidity, delusion, agitation.

KENAZ "cane-awes"
Reversed or Negative Meaning:
Insecurity, wishful thinking, lack of vision, stuck in a creative rut, breakup, instability, false hope, reassess.

WUNJO "woon-yo"
Reversed or Negative Meaning:
Sadness, hardship, separation, failure, feeling defeated, sorrow, alienation, impractical, stress, anxiety, troubles.

UPRIGHT **REVERSED**

PERTHRO "perth-row"
Reversed or Negative Meaning:
Sluggishness, loss of faith, abandonment, addiction, stagnation, loneliness, sexual frustration, letting go.

ALGIZ "all-yeese"
Reversed or Negative Meaning:
Hidden danger, warning, taboo, loss of faith, clouded vision, time for self-care, need to be more vigilant.

TEIWAZ "tee-whaz"
Reversed or Negative Meaning:
Lacking passion, imbalance, over-analysis, blocked energies, injustice, conflict, lack of motivation.

BERKANO "bear-kawn-oh"
Reversed or Negative Meaning:
Loss of control, being careless, having anxiety, family troubles, deceit, stagnation, blurred consciousness.

EHWAZ "aye-was"
Reversed or Negative Meaning:
Agitated, nervousness, instability, desire for change, doubt, disharmony, feeling restless, trust issues.

MANNAZ "man-awes"
Reversed or Negative Meaning:
Feeling isolated, depression, self-delusion, shyness, low self-esteem, misguided intuition, no help coming.

LAGUZ "law-goose"
Reversed or Negative Meaning:
Doubt or panic, misunderstanding, lack of creativity, confusion, fear, avoidance, obsession, blockages.

OTHALA "oath-awe-law"
Reversed or Negative Meaning:
Bigotry, bad karma, discrimination, prejudice, lack of order, poverty, homelessness, family argument, warning.

Now that we know which runes have negative meanings, we can look back at the example bindrune I created. Applying what we have learned in the previous chapter, let's see if we can spot any hidden reversed runes.

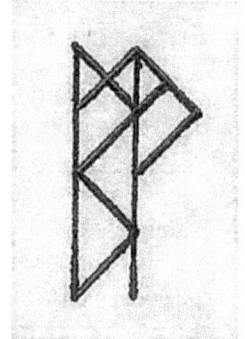

*The nine runes that do not have a reverse meaning have been faded out.

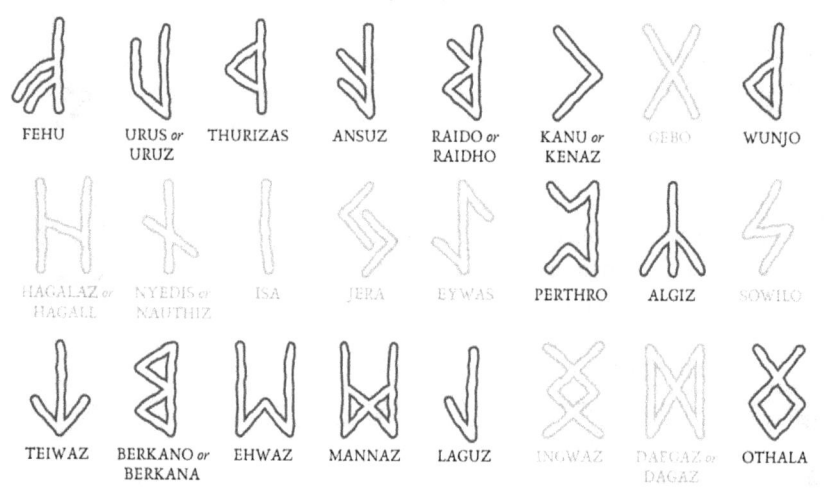

How many reversed runes can you find in the example bindrune? You should be able to find eight different reversed runes. Can you name all of them?

1._____

2._____

3._____

4._____

5._____

6._____

7._____

8._____

ANSWER ON PAGE 169

Not all 'negative' meanings are necessarily negative. For example, if you look at ALGIZ, one of the 'negative' interpretations states that you simply need to spend more time on self-care or be more vigilant to the world around you.

This could simply be interpreted as a nudge or hint from the universe, telling you that you are focusing all your energies on something mundane like a job. Or maybe you have a nurturing quality that likes to take care of other people when you should be taking time for yourself as well.

If you want to have the most substantial energy in your bindrune, the negative meanings should be considered throughout the design process. Not everyone utilizes the reversed runes in the same way, and there is no rule book saying that they must be used in this way either. If you do not believe in reversed rune meanings, then don't worry about it.

When all is said and done, your bindrune is yours. You will focus your energy on what you want to manifest with it, and it is entirely up to you how you want to create it. Do what feels right.

Using your favorite designs from earlier, let's determine how many hidden runes you have. On the next page, draw your favorite designs (your top two or three choices). Under each of your designs, write or draw out all of the reversed runes that you can find within that design. Feel free to also make notes of any negative or reversed meanings so you can get a better understanding of what you have created.

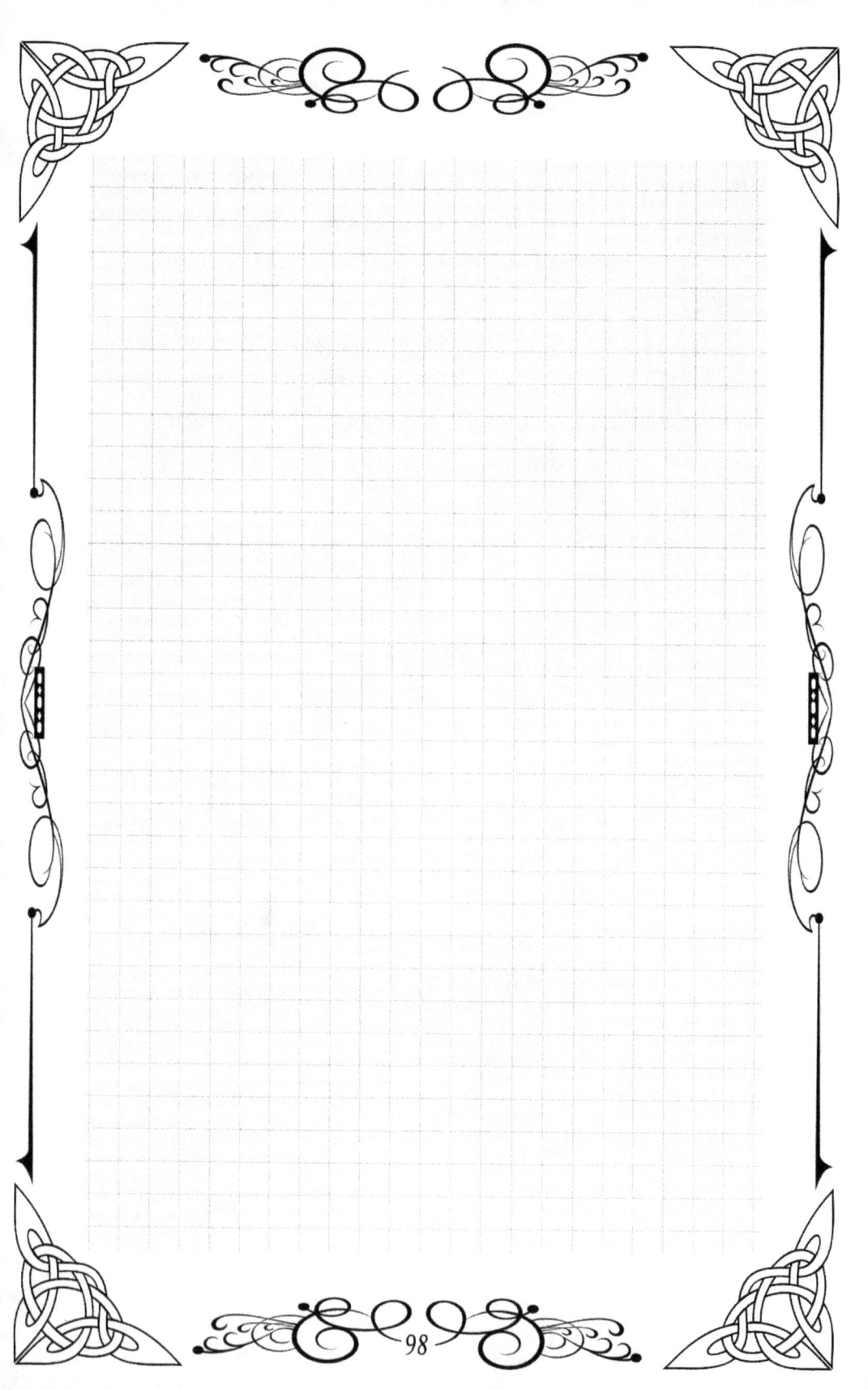

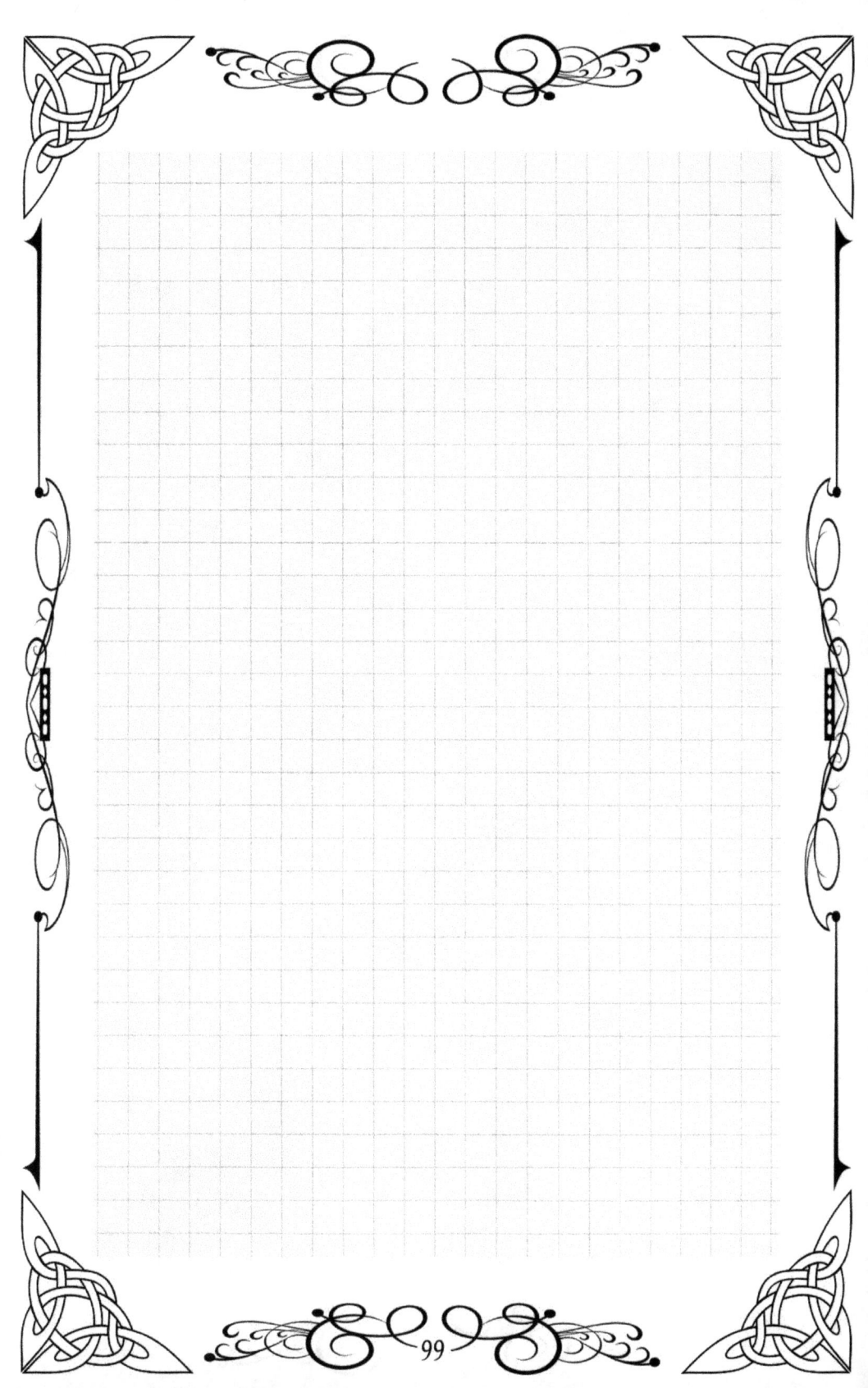

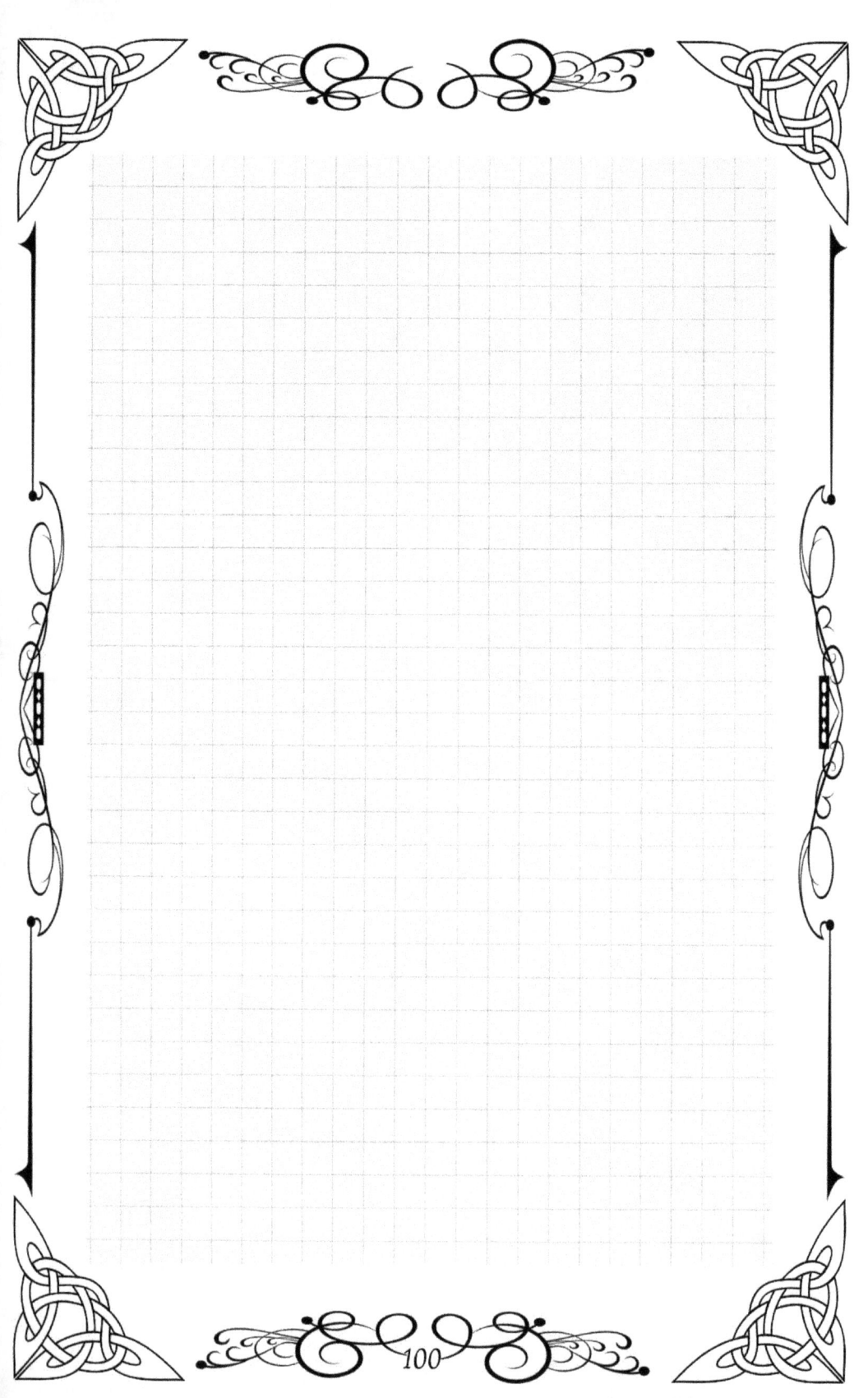

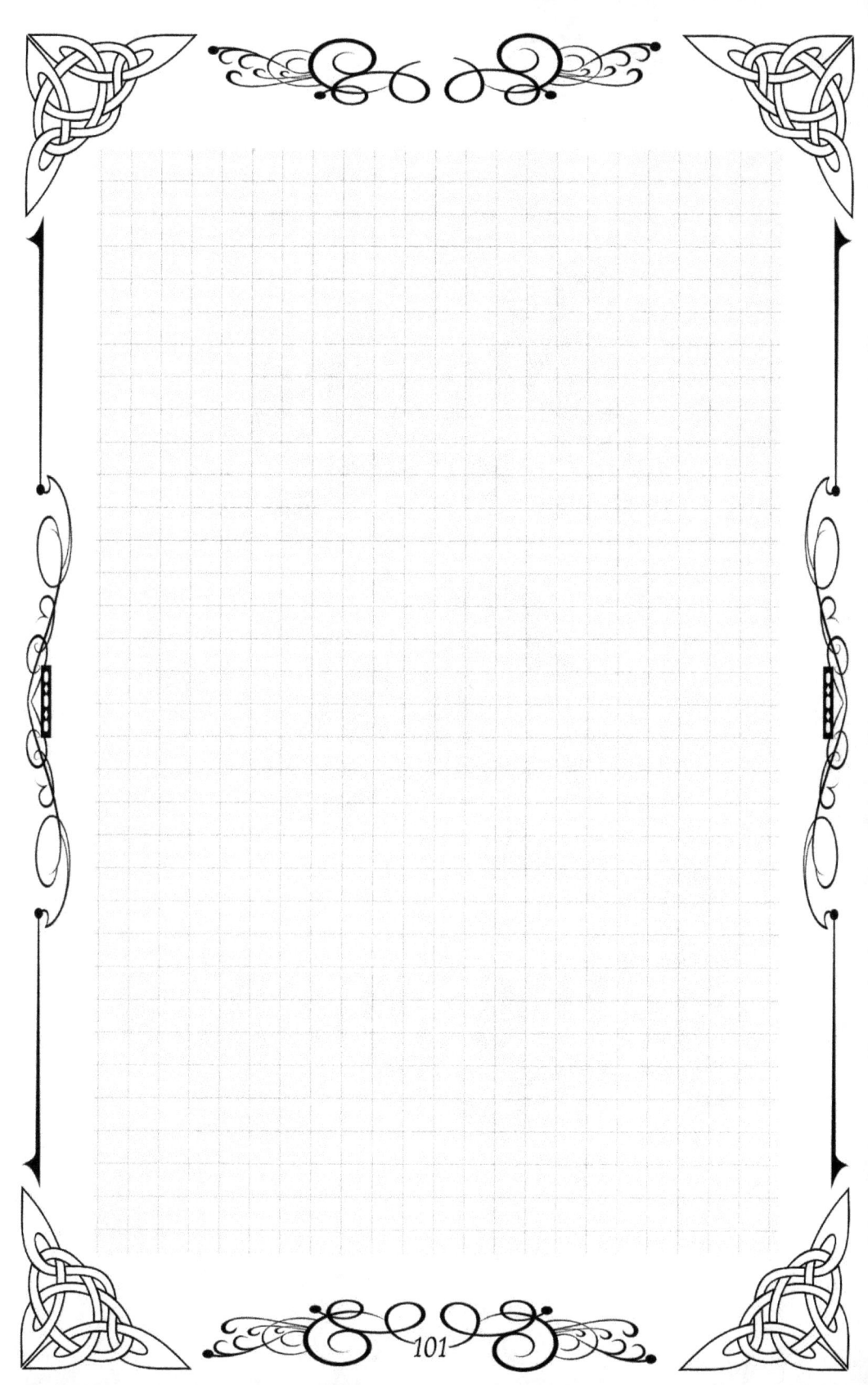

Making Final Adjustments

This is the step where you will be choosing your final bindrune design. Once you have spent some time in the creative process and have a few different creations that speak to you, it is time to review your composition and make any last-minute adjustments.

Have you gone through and identified any hidden runes? Are there any reversed runes that could negatively impact your energies? Have you determined if you would like to keep these alternate runes within your bindrune? Have you added any astrological or elemental symbols to strengthen your bindrune?

After carefully considering all the aspects, you can decide to remove certain concepts, hidden or reversed runes, and any other 'flaw' that you feel does not fit with the desired look you want to achieve.

At this point in the process, you can re-design, re-work, and re-create your bindrune to exclude any hidden or reversed energies that may have shown up. Use the following few pages to alter your design if needed or develop something entirely new to avoid negative energy.

If you need to go back and look for more hidden or reversed runes in your new design, then please do so. However, this process should not be rushed, and you must take your time to create a bindrune that is genuinely aligned with your intentions.

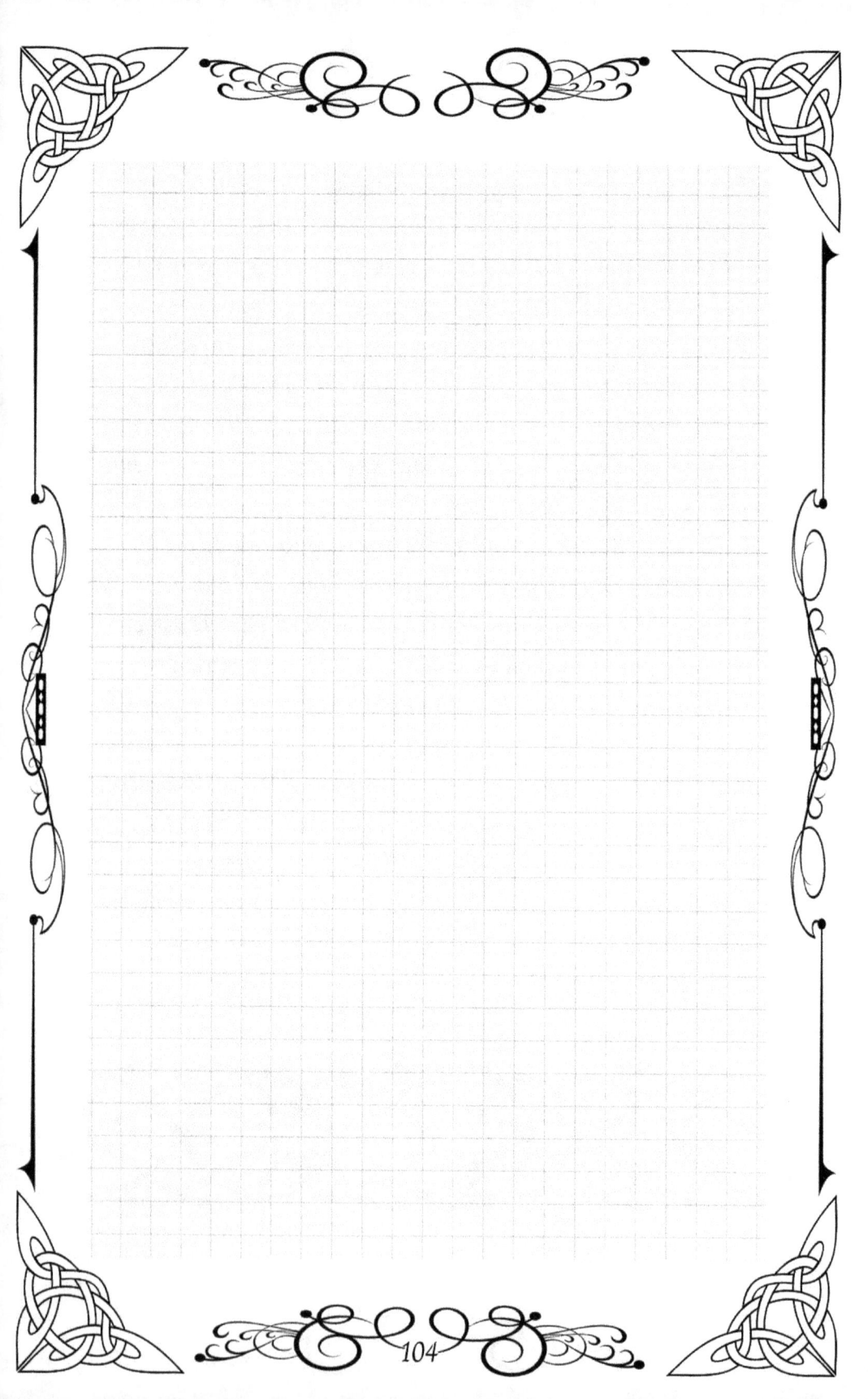

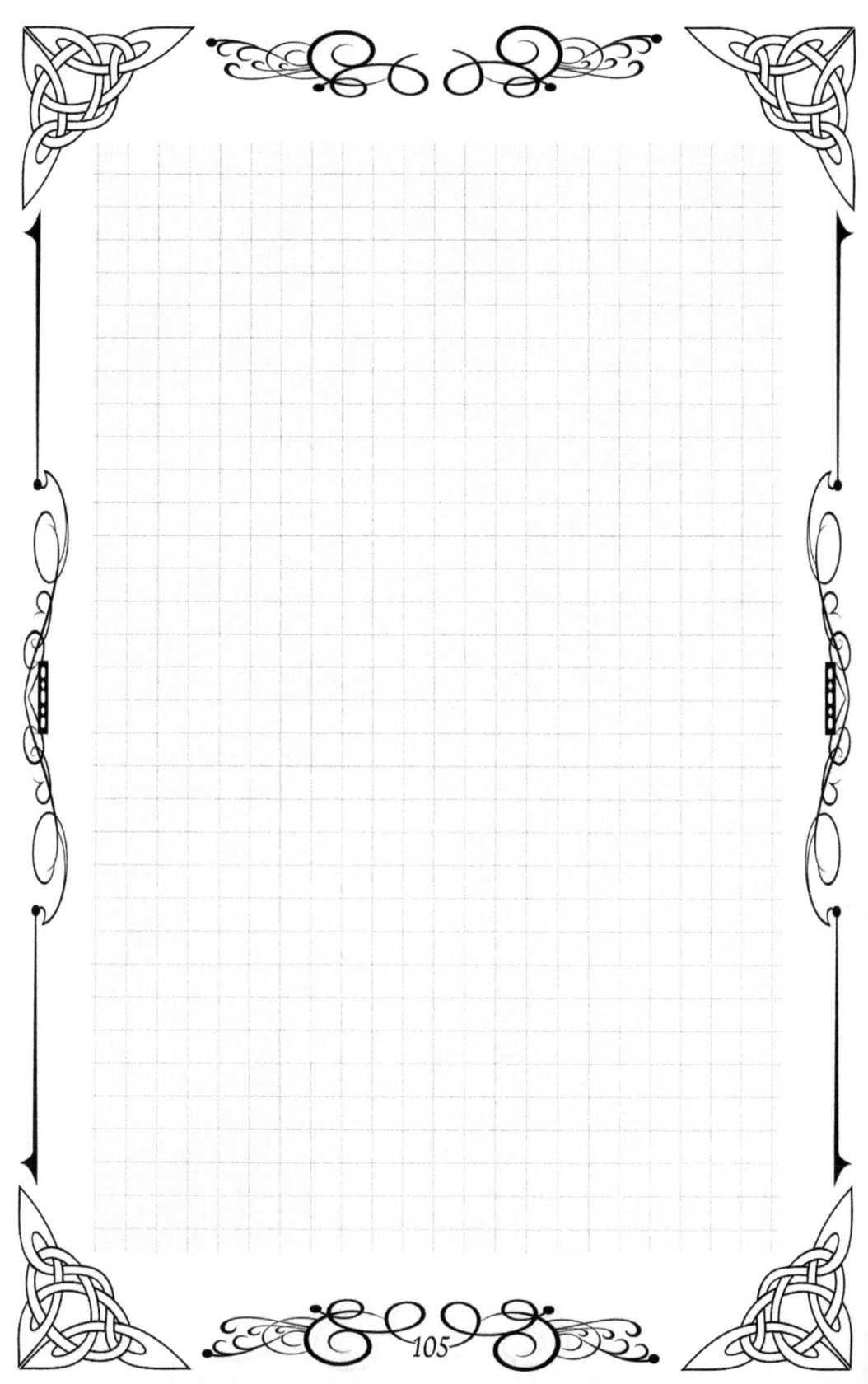

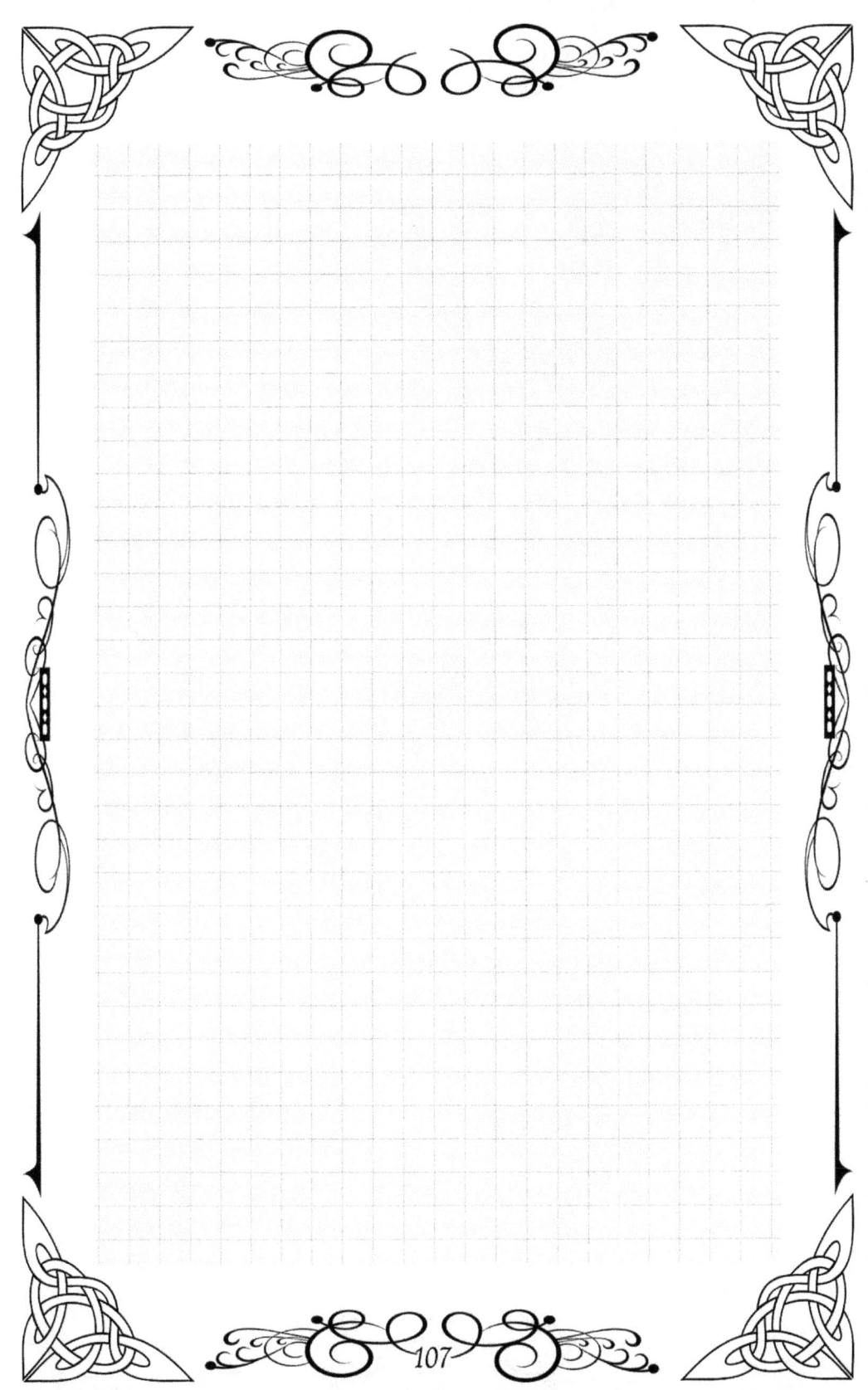

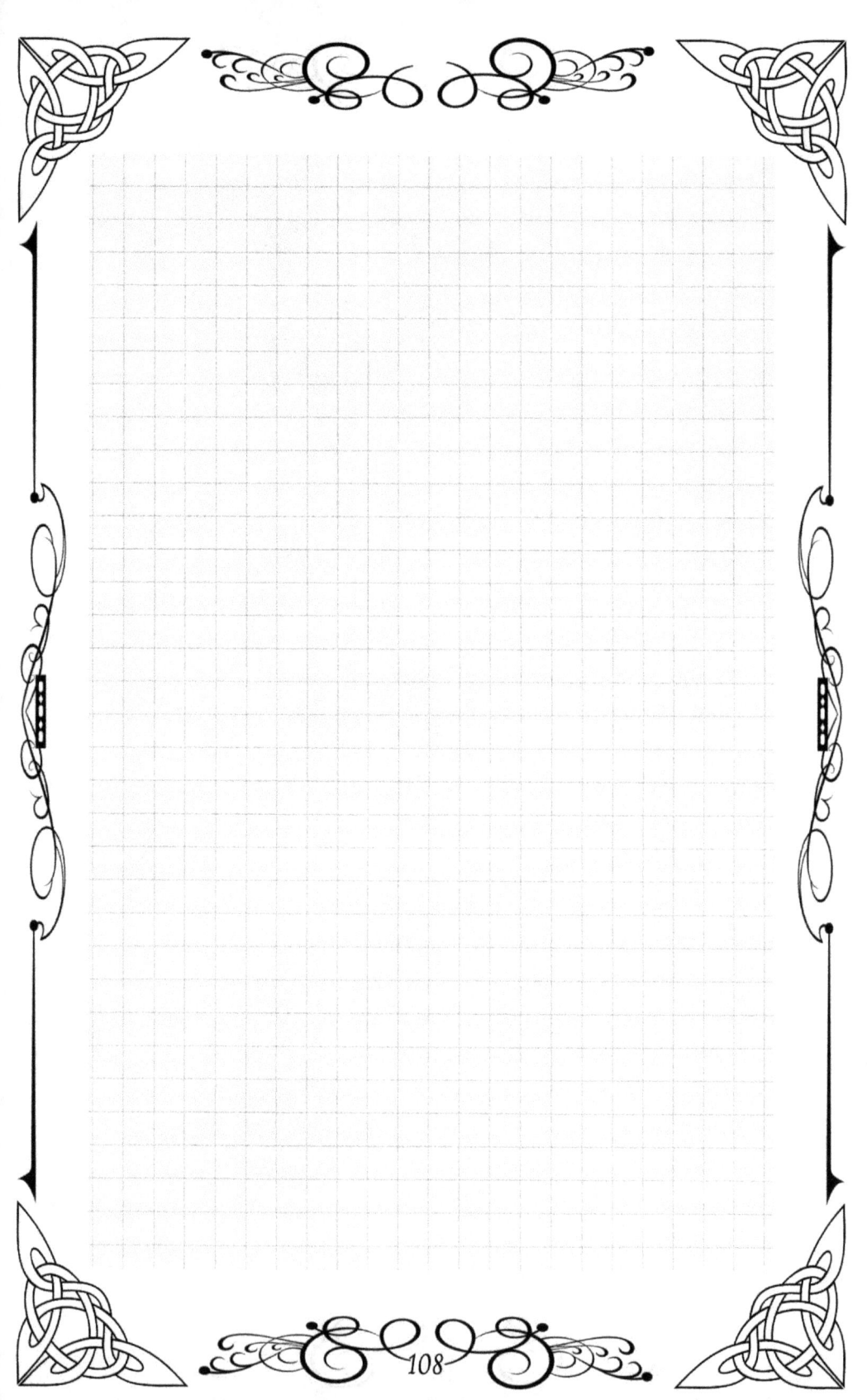

Completing and finalizing your Bindrune

Now that we have covered all the different areas of your bindrune design, you should have one creation that stands out the most.

Before we finalize your bindrune, we will go over a quick checklist to ensure that this is the bindrune you genuinely wish to use for manifesting. This list aims to make sure that you are 100% certain that you are happy with the bindrune you have created.

Be truthful to yourself when answering these questions. If you have any doubt about the design, this energy of doubt will transfer into the efficiency of your bindrune and hinder the manifesting process.

BINDRUNE CHECKLIST

- Does your chosen bindrune style compliment the vision you have for your manifesting intentions?
- Have you created your comprehensive list of intentions with their associated feelings?
- Have you read through all the runes and assigned them individually to your intentions and feelings?
- Do you have too many or too few runes in your design?
- Have you identified any hidden runes that may have appeared and considered their additional meanings?
- Have you identified any reversed runes and the potential negative energies that they bring?
- Did you change your design to eliminate any of these hidden or reversed runes?
- It is not necessary, but have you incorporated any zodiac or elemental symbols into your design?
- Do you feel connected and happy with your final design?

If any of the questions make you doubt whether or not you have a powerful bindrune, I would suggest going back, taking your time, and drawing out some new ideas until you have your 'this is it' moment.

If you feel that you are in a creative rut, take some time away, go for a walk, take a deep breath, and come back to it later because the process can be a little overwhelming at times.

Once you are 100% happy and feel connected with your completed design, it is time to clean it up and make a final draft for the next step.

There are many different methods that people like to use when finalizing their bind rune. If you prefer to draw out an exact copy on paper using a ruler to ensure that all the lines are straight, then go for it. If you know how to use a digital program like Paint or Canva, you can make a digital copy of your final bindrune as well.

This final copy will be the template to follow when you get to the next chapter, Selecting the Material for your Bindrune.

Selecting the Material for your Bindrune

We have now taken several steps in the preparation of exercising your 'will' in the manifesting work that you have initiated. You have just completed the central and most important process, which was taking the time to create your bindrune, and by doing so, you have focused your energy, intentions, and desires into an immensely influential amulet or sigil.

Creating a bindrune is no simple task, as it involves focus, concentration, energy, and a strong desire to bring forth positive change in your life. However, you should feel very proud of what you have accomplished and what you have done up to this point.

- You have taken the time to write down your intentions and the feelings they bring you,
- Chosen runes to represent those feelings,
- Determined if the hidden or reversed runes were beneficial or unfavorable,
- Added your desired zodiac or elemental symbols,
- Created and possibly edited your design,
- Finalized a bindrune that is authentically representative of what you wish to manifest.

I would like you to take a moment, close your eyes, and think about everything you have accomplished up to this point and how that makes you feel. So please take a minute, sit with those feelings, and be mindful of how they make you feel. This is a great feeling, isn't it?

Keeping that feeling of happiness, you can now select the material that will hold your completed bindrune.

You can virtually use any material, but it is the intent of your bindrune that you need to consider and what it is meant to do. Two important things to remember are:

A) How long do you intend to keep your bindrune? If it is a short-term goal, then paper could work best. If it is a long-term goal, then paper may not be the best option as it will deteriorate over time, and

B) Are you going to display the bindrune or carry it with you? This step is necessary because a bindrune that is meant to help you save money would most likely be kept in your wallet, so a giant plaque or wooden disk would not make very much sense in this situation.

Think about how your bindrune would best serve its purpose. For example, if you created it as a protection amulet, having it on a material such as leather, wood, or stone to hang or display somewhere within your home would be ideal. This would mean that your bindrune needs to be visually attractive and reasonably permanent.

If your bindrune is meant to protect you during travel, then using a smaller 'travel size' material would be your best option in this instance if you need to carry it with you or place it in your vehicle.

The material that you choose to contain your bindrune should be something that you are energetically connected with.

To help you decide which material would work best for your bindrune, I have included a list of the most common objects and their meanings. However, if you already know which component you would like to use, trust your intuition and the guidance from the universe.

Material Correspondences

FABRICS

Canvas: Creativity, new beginnings, potential, possibilities.
Cotton: Simplicity, harvest, protection, rain, good luck.
Denim: Ruggedness, durability, independence, rebellion.
Felt: Protection, good luck, wealth (white felt), sacrifice, strength.
Hemp: Travel, vision, enlightenment, opening gates or doors.
Lace: Sacredness, a rite of passage, feminine energy, privilege, sensuality, sexuality, duality.
Leather: Protection, covering, animal energy, instinct.
Linen: Righteousness, purity, rest, elegance, luxury, light and purity, wealth.
Satin: Lustrous, sensual, shine, love.
Silk: Wealth, prestige, transformation, magical insulation.
Velvet: Distinction, emotions, royalty, leadership.
Wool: Hope, renewal, durability, comfort, warmth.

FABRIC CORRESPONDENCES

Aries: Lamb's wool.
Taurus: Leather.
Gemini: Gauze, chiffon, voile.
Cancer: Flannel.
Leo: Lamé, brocade, velvet.
Virgo: Cotton, canvas, chintz.
Libra: Silk, satin.
Scorpio: Snakeskin.
Sagittarius: Spandex, lycra.
Capricorn: Mohair, cashmere, hemp.
Aquarius: Feathers, metallic fabrics.
Pisces: Rayon, nylon, watermarked taffeta.

Earth: Leather, wool, cotton, felt.
Air: Chiffon, voile, gauze.
Fire: Satin, lace, velvet.
Water: silk, satin, taffeta.
Spirit: Hemp, linen, felt.

TYPES OF WOOD

Apple: Grounded, bountiful, abundance, spiritual connection, fertility, goddess, healing, honor, health, love.

Ash: Highly intuitive, protective, guidance, healing, clearing of a path, courage, reverence, confidence, induce prophetic dreams.

Aspen: Protective, cleansing, energetic, helps aid in moving forward, healing, purification, wishes, stress relief.

Birch: Purifying, cleansing, grounding, renewal, fresh starts, protection for children.

Cedar: Excellent for divination and purification.
California Redwood: Healing energy, endurance, balance, grounding.

Cypress: Soothing, calming, positive, protection, consecration.

Elm: Cycles, beginnings and endings, protective.

Elder: Protection for negative energy, Intelligence, understanding, working with the fey, healing.

Hazel: Protection, leadership, mental acuity, fertility, insight.

Maple: Spiritual, centering, great for beginners, animal and nature magic, family bonds, healthy relationships.

Mahogany: New beginnings, fertility, useful in energy work, strong bonds, and helpful in moving forward.

Oak: Strong grounding energy, spiritual, highly protective, masculine, focus, balance, great for beginners, increase intuition, physical and emotional strength, working with the fey.

TYPES OF WOOD

Poplar: Fluid, water, spirit, diverse energy, brings out softer masculine qualities.

Teak: Magical, strong-willed, genuine, highly feminine, protective, healing.

Walnut: Well balanced, magickal, companion, strong bond, grounding, stabilizing, calming, protective, highly energetic, prosperity, abundance, healing.

Willow: Feminine, earth, spirit, enchanting, works well with lunar and moon magick, drawing down blessings from the moon, wishes.

Yew: Masculine, reincarnation, works well for divination, scrying, and cross-realm communication. Protective.

WOOD CORRESPONDENCES

Aries: Alder, Willow, Sycamore, Cypress.

Taurus: Willow, Hawthorn, Beech, Rosewood, Pine, Spruce.

Gemini: Hawthorn, Oak, Dogwood, Elm, Holly, Reed, Spruce, Walnut.

Cancer: Oak, Holly, English Oak, Ivy, Larch, Rosewood.

Leo: Holly, Hazel, Ash, Dogwood, Hornbeam, Pear, Poplar, Silver Lime, Spruce.

Virgo: Hazel, Vine, Apple, Ebony, Chestnut, Hornbeam, Pear.

Libra: Vine, Ivy, Beech, Birch, Olive, Rosewood.

Scorpio: Ivy, Reed, Ebony, English Oak, Fir.

Sagittarius: Reed, Elder, Maple, Sycamore, Walnut.

WOOD CORRESPONDENCES

Capricorn: Elder, Birch, Acacia, Cedar, Elm, Larch, Pine.

Aquarius: Birch, Rowan, Apple, Cedar, Ebony, English Oak, Pear, Red Oak.

Pisces: Rowan, Ash, Birch, Laurel, Silver Lime, Willow, Vine.

Earth: Ash, Elm, Hawthorn, Cypress, Honeysuckle, Lilac.

Air: Aspen, Alder, Birch, Ash, Beech, Acacia, Almond, Hazel, Maple, Pine.

Fire: Thorn, Holly, Oak, Alder, Ash, Cedar, Maple, Walnut, Rowan, Mahogany, Juniper, Fig.

Water: Alder, Hazel, Willow, Magnolia, Apple, Birch, Elder, Elm, Rose.

Spirit: Mistletoe and Almond.

Clearing Negative Energy

When you are working with your chosen material, it is always wise to remove any negative energies that may be trapped within. You would not want any misaligned powers to alter your intentions, do you?

For materials such as fabric and wood, the easiest way to clear these negative energies would be to pass your material through the smoke of a sage smudge stick or Palo Santo incense, which is known to banish and clear away any negative energies.

CRYSTALS & GEMSTONES

Because there is a wide variety of crystals and gemstones which could fill an entire book, I will include my top ten choices here, which are great for beginners and experienced practitioners alike.

You can find plenty of resources explaining in detail all the different crystals and gemstones you could use for your bindrunes. Use this list as a starting point to build your knowledge as you advance on your journey.

Amethyst: De-stressing, purifies the aura, brings divine wisdom, relaxation, generates gentle vibrations, aids in a sound sleep when placed next to the bed at night, helps to keep you calm throughout the day when you have a small amethyst in your pocket.

Clear Quartz: Reduce negativity, improves mood and mental clarity, unblocks energy flows. Clear Quartz is a 'programmable' crystal used for intention-setting work, amplifying energies, and being a powerful healer.

Rose Quartz: Tenderness, compassion, comfort, peace, helps to feel the confidence of the goddess inside you, bring new love into your life, strengthen existing love. When placed in the heart of the home, it will tighten family bonds.

Smoky Quartz: Great for meditation as it grounds you through your root chakra, harmony, balance, connection to the spiritual world while keeping you safe in this one, release negative energies.

Selenite: White light energy, soothing, cleansing, purifying, clears out negative energy, making you feel instantly more positive, useful in opening and closing energy circles.

CRYSTALS & GEMSTONES

Green Aventurine: Deep healing, nature, new life, regrowth, brings new opportunities, good luck, practical when placed in your palm during meditation to clear energy blockages.

Black Tourmaline: Cleansing and purifying, reduces anxiety, pushes away any unwanted negative energy or people, highly protective and helpful to use as wards around the home. Absorbs electromagnetic radiation from electronics.

Moonstone: Balancing, new beginnings, helps to promote inner strength and growth, soothes emotional instability, calming, helps to promote love, enhances intuition, inspiration, success, good fortune in business.

Citrine: Good luck, money, wealth, great for boosting the energy of surrounding crystals, helpful in manifesting, abundance, and prosperity. Raises self-esteem, helps in overcoming depression, releases negative feelings and anger.

Pyrite (Fools Gold): Ultimate good luck charm, helps you to see the path ahead, sun energy, healing, good fortune, abundance, brings professional success when placed on your desk or work area, channels good fortune into your life if placed near a window.

CRYSTALS & GEMSTONES CORRESPONDENCES

Aries: Amethyst, Rose Quartz, Carnelian.

Taurus: Green Jade, Rose Quartz, Emerald, Smoky Quartz.

Gemini: Green Jade, Tiger's Eye.

Cancer: Opalite, Citrine, Moonstone.

Leo: Tiger's Eye, Citrine, Garnet, Clear Quartz.

Virgo: Green Jade, Citrine, Red Jasper.

Libra: Opalite, Rose Quartz, Bloodstone.

Scorpio: Rose Quartz, Black Obsidian, Malachite, Clear Quartz.

Sagittarius: Sodalite, Black Obsidian, Lepidolite.

Capricorn: Sodalite, Tiger's Eye, Fluorite.

Aquarius: Amethyst, Fluorite, Aquamarine, Hematite.

Pisces: Amethyst, Fluorite, Clear Quartz.

Earth: Moss Agate, Black Tourmaline, Jet, Malachite, Emerald, Peridot, Jasper, Onyx, Petrified Wood, Halite.

Air: Tiger's Eye, Opal, Citrine, Topaz, Turquoise, Rhodonite, Amazonite, Fluorite, Calcite.

Fire: Carnelian, Sun Stone, Red Calcite, Amber, Garnet, Tektites, Ruby, Fire Agate, Red Jasper, Citrine.

Water: Amethyst, Pearls, Aquamarine, Coral, Moonstone, Azurite, Blue Agate, Chalcedony, Lapis Lazuli, Sodalite.

Spirit: Clear Quartz, Danburite, Petalite, Amethyst, Spodumene.

Clearing Negative Energy

When clearing negative energy from crystals and gemstones, there are various ways this can be achieved. The following are my top five methods to clearing, cleansing, and charging your crystals before you apply your bindrune.

Running Water: Like a stream or river, neutralize any negative energies and return them to the earth. Natural running water is best, but you can rinse your crystals under your faucet for the same effect. Be sure that your stone is completely submerged for at least a minute. Pat dry.
*Not recommended for soft or brittle stones such as Selenite, Kyanite, and Halite.

Salt Water: Salt is widely known to absorb unwanted energy and banish negativity. Natural seawater (saltwater) would work best, but you can also add household salt to a bowl of water to achieve the same outcome. Completely submerge your stones for a few hours or up to a few days. Rinse and pat dry.
*Not recommended for soft, porous stones or containing trace metals, such as Malachite, Selenite, Halite, Calcite, Lepidolite, and Angelite.

Brown Rice: Fill a bowl with dry brown rice. Bury your stone(s) entirely beneath the rice and leave it to cleanse for 24 hours. The rice will absorb any negativity from your crystals or gemstones, especially for any protective stones such as Black Tourmaline. Dispose of the rice immediately after cleansing.
*This method can be used for any type of crystal or gemstone.

Clearing Negative Energy

Moon Light: Heavily centered around the lunar cycles, one vastly popular method to cleanse crystals is moonlight. This is typically done during a full moon, as this is the most energetic time; however, you can cleanse and charge your crystals at any point.

Place your stone on a windowsill that faces the direction of the moon. Try to get your crystals in place during dusk, when the sun is about to set completely, and the moonlight will start to fill the night sky.

If you are able to place your stone directly on the earth, this will add additional cleansing and charging properties to your crystals. Just be sure that they will not be disturbed by animals or other humans.

Leave your stones overnight for approximately 8 – 12 hours. Be sure to remove your stones in the morning, so they are not sitting in direct sunlight. Rinse off your stones and pat dry.

*Not recommended for softer stones such as Celestite, Halite, and Selenite.

Sage: Sage is believed to be a sacred plant that has a multitude of healing properties. To clear inharmonious energy from your crystals and restore their natural powers, pass them through sage smoke.

If you cannot cleanse outdoors, be sure that you are near an open window to disperse the smoke and negative energies. Also, make sure to have a fire-safe bowl on hand if you need to burn any loose sage. Pass your crystals through the sage smoke for approximately 30 - 60 seconds per stone.

*This method can be used for any type of crystal or gemstone.

Selecting the Material for your Bindrune

Now that we have covered a generous selection of materials and how to clear away negative energy, it is time to make your choice.

While you are contemplating the choice for your material, there is also the matter of choosing which 'writing implement' you will be utilizing to place your bindrune on your chosen material.

Keep in mind that the material will play a huge factor in what kind of writing tool you can or cannot use, but there are always choices. Start by looking through the stationary you currently have. Do you prefer to use permanent markers, pens, pencils, or crayons? What about some thread and a needle to sew your design? Would any of these work on your bindrune material?

If you are a creative or artistic individual, you can also paint your bindrune. You may also consider a different path, such as wood-burning kits, oils, pen and ink, charcoal, pastels, or even a highlighter. Carving your bindrune onto the material with a knife or carving tool (I personally like to use my electric Dremel carving tool) will ensure a permanent amulet that will not fade or weaken with time.

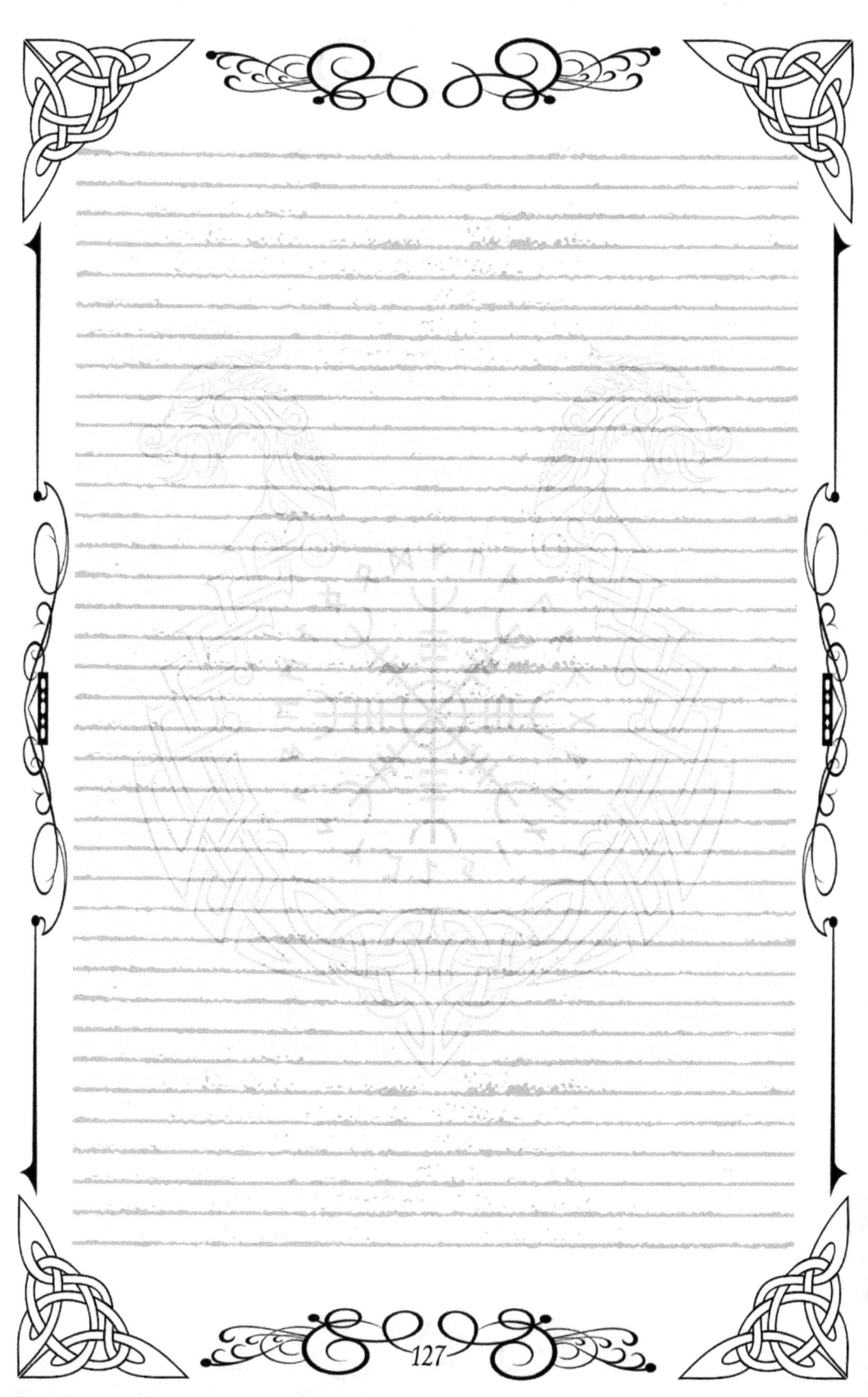

The Creation Ritual

THE CREATION RITUAL

"You are the master of your destiny. You can influence, direct, and control your own environment. You can make your life what you want it to be." - Napoleon Hill

You have your final bindrune design, your chosen material, and writing implement. Now you get to create the physical bindrune into existence for your manifesting desires.

If we refer to Create a Personal Ritual (Page 59), we will again look at how you can build a ritual space to create your bindrune. There are many different methods to establish a safe ritual space, but this depends on your specific circumstances and available time.

The Creation Ritual and how formal you wish to make it is entirely up to you. Some individuals prefer to practice in a 'highly ritualized' space as this provides a focus for your intentions. However, you may not be able to do this as your working space may be too small, or it could be inappropriate to pull out the candles and incense in your current location.

Depending on your time and space available, however meticulous or informal you wish your ritual to be, it is most important to remember that you will be focusing your intent and will into the bindrune you are making.

Start by establishing your ritual space. If this involves calling the quarters, lighting candles, burning some sage, calling the god and goddess, and meditating to ground your energy, then go ahead and do that now.

THE CREATION RITUAL

If the only thing you can do is meditate, then this is also okay. The main thing you need to accomplish is to have a space to focus and work on your bindrune without any distractions.

Next, you will lay out your material and the writing implement of your choice (whether it be a pen, marker, ink, thread and needle, knife, or carving tool). Finally, with materials ready and intentions clear, you will start creating your bindrune and giving your amulet its power!

Your bindrune may be one complete shape, but it is essential that when you start to draw or carve your design, you need to focus on each symbol instead of just the entire shape. Your bindrune is a combination of runes, and you will need to focus your intentions on each rune as you are placing them on the material.

As you focus on each rune, zodiac, or elemental symbol, think about how it fits with the other ones in your design and how they interconnect. In addition, it is recommended that you chant the name of the rune, zodiac, or element as you are carving or drawing them, as this further helps to focus your energies during the creation process.

After you have finished drawing of carving each symbol, culminating in the completion of your bindrune, it is time to sit and meditate with it. While meditating, focus on the shape, the individual symbols, and your intentions for what you want this bindrune to achieve for you.

Throughout the process of creating your bindrune, you have focused your intentions and put in a large amount of energy. Just looking at your finished bindrune should give you an immense feeling of happiness and pride. Your bindrune should be treated with reverence.

THE CREATION RITUAL

When you feel that you have successfully meditated and imbued your energies into the bindrune, it is time to close your ritual space.

Some practitioners choose to make offerings to the God Odin, thanking him for using the runes and any other Gods or Goddesses that may have been part of your ritual. If this is something you would not typically practice, it may be something to consider, but it is not a deal-breaker. It will not change your bindrune energies.

Now that you have created your bindrune and closed your ritual space, the entire process is completed, right? Wrong! You have made a focal point for your intentions, thoughts, and desires, but the magickal work continues.

Next, we will be discussing how to Activate your Bindrune so that you can start the manifesting transformation in your life.

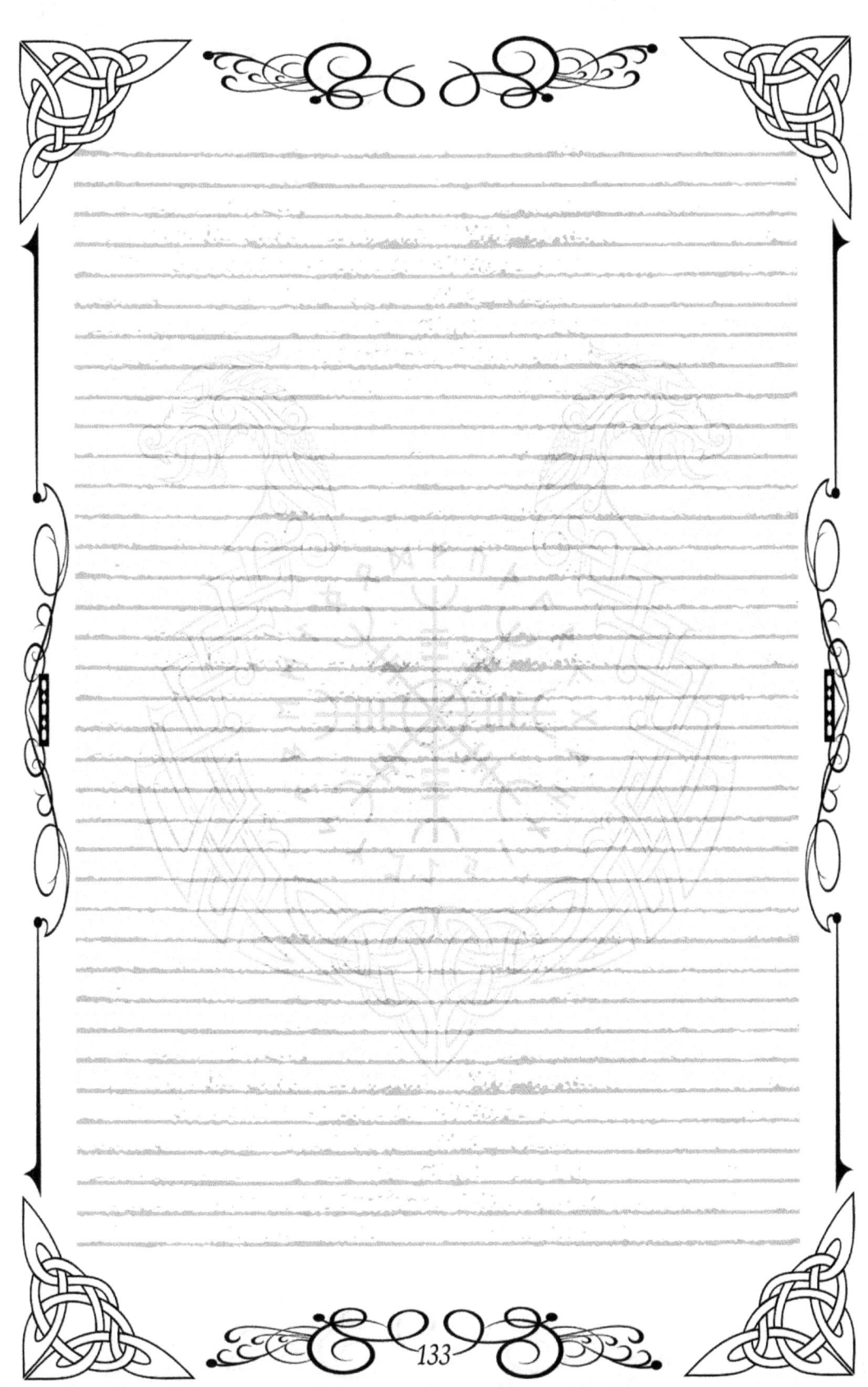

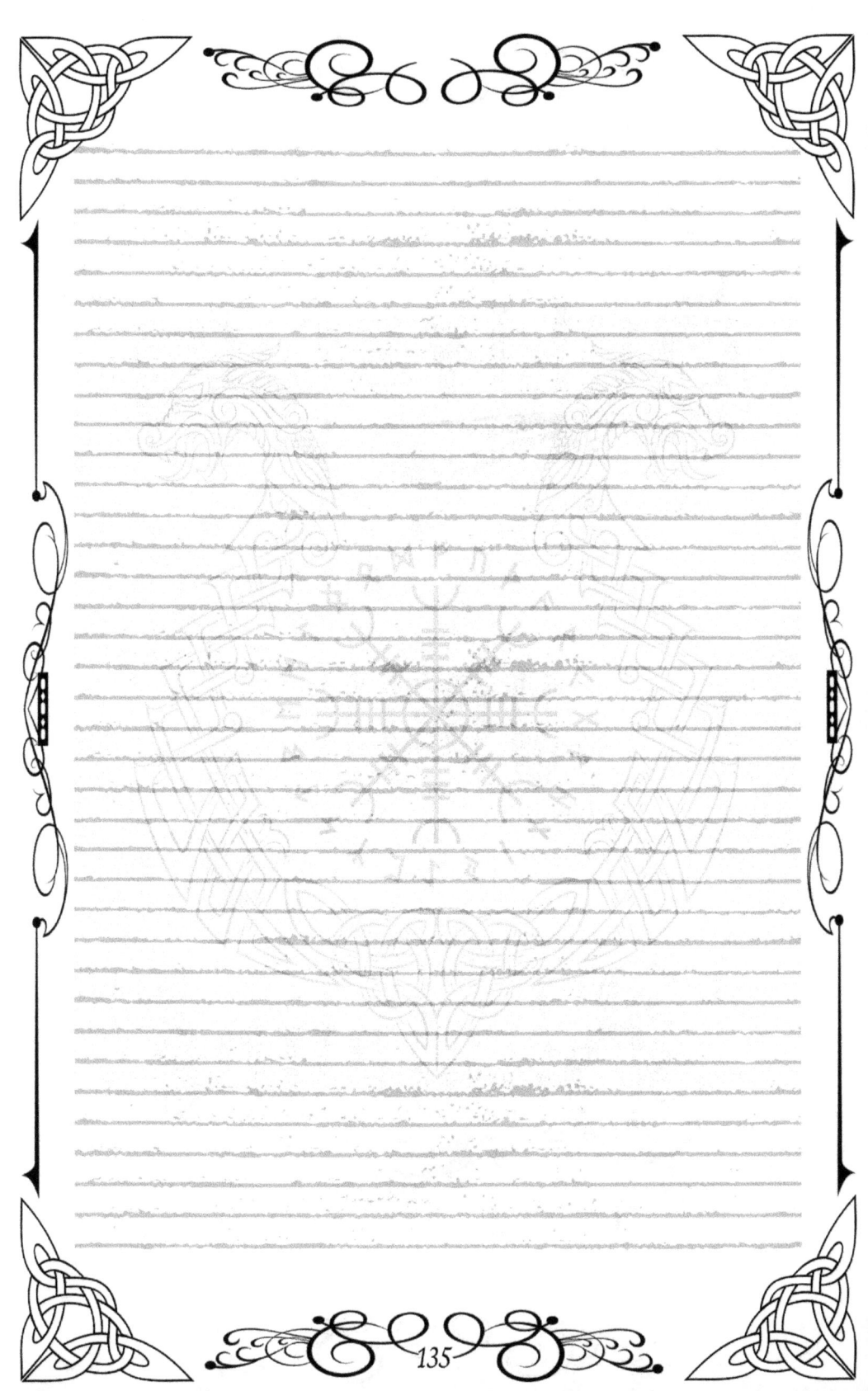

Activating your Bindrune

Activation can be a fun activity because you get to choose how you would like to switch on your finished bindrune before using it for manifesting.

I will share some of my most favorite practices for activating my bindrunes. Feel free to use whatever feels suitable for you and your manifesting purposes. Essentially, you need to focus on the energy you wish to instill within your bindrune for each of these techniques.

ELEMENTAL ACTIVATION

Earth: To activate your bindrune, simply bury your amulet in the ground for a day and a night. Be sure that it will not be disturbed by animals or other humans. When activation is complete, rinse off your bindrune and pat dry before use.

Air: Activation can be achieved by passing your amulet through the smoke of your favorite incense or sage smudge. Alternatively, you can also set your amulet outdoors on a windy day for a few hours to let the air activate it. Be sure to secure it in place, so it does not blow away on you.

Fire: Depending on the type of material you chose for your bindrune, a fire could potentially be a damaging or dangerous activation technique. Fire is a powerful element in and of itself, so please exercise caution if you are using this method.

The easiest and most effective practice would be to use your favorite candle. *BE CAREFUL NOT TO BURN YOURSELF* Light the candle and let it burn for a minute or two. Then, with your amulet in your dominant hand, carefully pass it through the flame while imagining that the energy of the fire is 'activating' your bindrune.

Alternatively, if you do not wish to use physical fire or flame, you can set out your bindrune on a sunny day to absorb the fire energy from the sun.

Water: To activate your bindrune, simply place it in a bowl of water for up to 12 hours. On the other hand, if you have moon water, this can also be an amazingly effective and powerful way to activate your bindrune. Be aware that if you are using certain crystals, water can be damaging. Pat dry when complete.

ASTROLOGICAL ACTIVATION

Activating your bindrune by astrological means can be tricky. This involves knowing where the constellations are in the night sky to have maximum effect. But fear not; you do not need to study an astrological chart to activate your amulet properly.

For the most straightforward method, all you must do is place your charm outside on a clear night under the starry sky. If there is a full moon, even better. It may take some research into your local weather forecast to find out which night would be ideal for you to accomplish this. Then, place your bindrune somewhere safe after the sun has set, and be sure to retrieve it before the sun rises in the morning.

For an extra power boost for your activation, you can also wait until your birthday. In the evening on your birthday, place your bindrune outside under the night sky after the sun has set, and again, retrieve it before the sun comes up. Although the position of the stars and constellations shift over time, the night sky on your birthday will be relatively the same as when you were born, therefore bringing immense personal energy and power to this day and night.

BREATHING LIFE ACTIVATION

Breathwork can be a very effective cleansing practice by 'blowing' the negativity away from a material or crystal. Equally efficient, 'breathing life' into your bindrune is just as powerful when activating your amulet.

To start, place your bindrune in your dominant hand. Focus strongly on the intentions, desires, and dreams that you wish to manifest in your life.

Inhaling through your nose, bring the bindrune closer to your mouth, and with short, forceful breaths, imagine your vital life-force energy being absorbed into the bindrune with each blow. You can do this for as long as you feel necessary, focusing only on your intentions and energy with each breath.

MEDITATION & VISUALIZATION ACTIVATION

If you enjoy working with the deep calm that meditating provides, this method might work best for you. Play some soft music or nature sounds in the background to help you get into a suitable space.

Meditate as you usually would be comfortable, ground your energies, and relax your entire body. When you feel that you have achieved a true meditative state, take your bindrune in the palm of both hands and gently rest them comfortably on your lap.

With your eyes closed, take deep breaths in through your nose and out through your mouth. With each breath in, visualize a bright white light entering your body. This light is purifying and cleansing. Visualize this light removing any doubt or worry you have.

Continue to relax as you visualize this light throughout your body. When you feel the moment is right, using your mind, start to move this light through your body, down your arms, and into your bindrune. Imagine that this divine energy is being absorbed into your amulet through your hands to activate your manifesting desires.

When you feel that your bindrune has been sufficiently energized, bring yourself back to a conscious state of mind and place your amulet in a safe place until you are ready to use it.

CRYSTAL & GEMSTONE ACTIVATION

If you love to use crystals and gemstones in your daily practice, activating your bindrune in this manner could be extremely powerful for you. This method can be used on any material, but the energies would be most potent if your bindrune were on a crystal itself.

Since the crystals you work with regularly already carry so much of your power within them, using these in an 'activation grid' for your bindrune would be highly beneficial for you. This approach has the same principles as a crystal grid if you are familiar with using these.

Crystal grids are available in many different shapes and sizes, with their designs being reminiscent of the sacred geometry in mandalas. These grids are typically crafted on cloth or wooden materials.

Following is a small sample of popular crystal grid designs that are widely used throughout the world. I have also provided a couple full page crystal grids for you to use if you do not have access to one.

CRYSTAL GRIDS & SACRED GEOMETRY

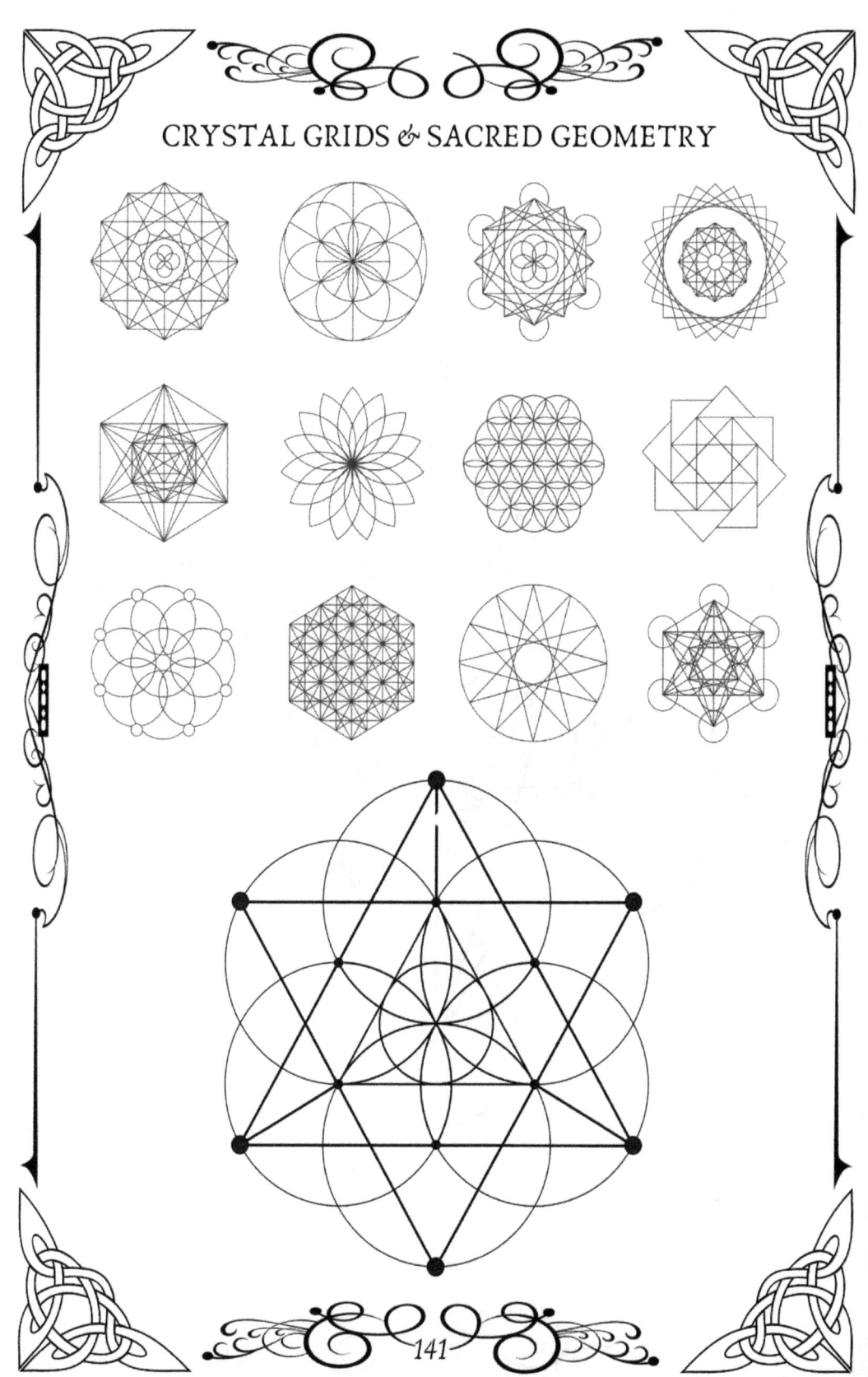

CRYSTAL GRIDS & SACRED GEOMETRY

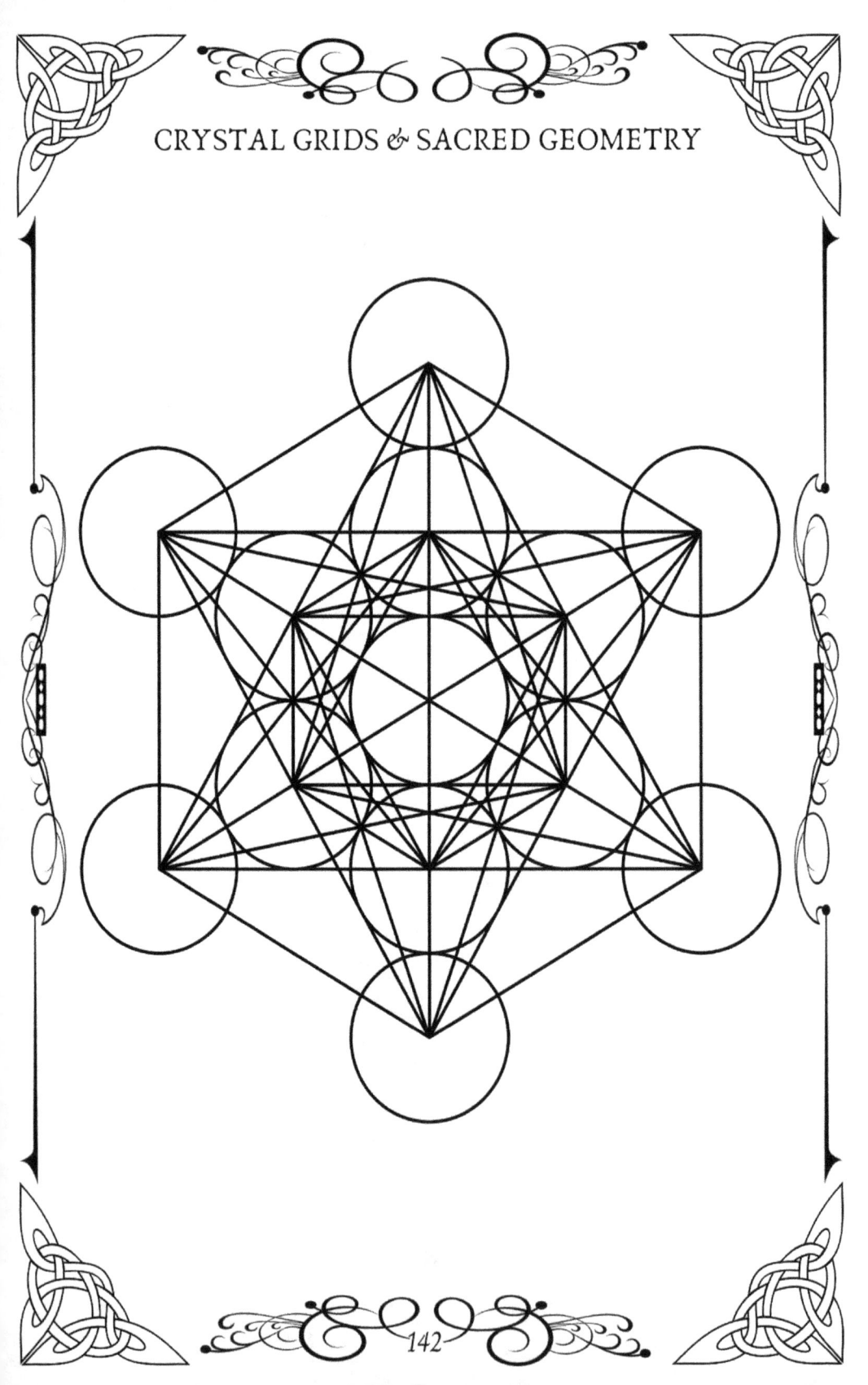

CRYSTAL GRIDS & SACRED GEOMETRY

 Depending on your available supplies, you may not own one of these beautifully intricate crystal grids. In that case, these can be easily obtained from many different artisans or retailers online.

 Alternatively, if you are feeling a spark of artistic inclination, you can always create your own as well. To make things much simpler for the beginner bindrune user, another crystal grid 'formation' that you are most likely familiar with is the Pentagram.

The Pentagram, or Pentacle, would be the most accessible symbol to recreate if you have time restrictions. However, this can also be just as effective if drawn on a piece of paper for the use of your bindrune activation.

Once you have your crystal grid or Pentagram ready to go, we will activate your bindrune. Both the Pentagram and the more complex grid designs will be used in the same manner, and it just depends on what you have available to you and your personal preference.

The number of crystals you will be working with depends on your chosen grid's outer points. With your bindrune in the grid center, you will place a crystal on each of the outlying points to create a circle. The center point holding your bindrune will absorb the power and energy from the surrounding crystals.

The first thing you need to do is establish how many crystals you need and which ones you will use. Every crystal has diverse energy and meaning, so it may take some research to find which ones will work best with your intentions.

The goal is to surround your bindrune so that it can absorb and bask in all the other vibrations around it. Some popular choices for grid activation include, but are not limited to, Clear Quartz, Selenite, Carnelian, Kyanite, Apophyllite, and your birthstone.

Once you have decided on which stones you will be using, start your activation by clearing your mind and meditating for a few minutes to focus your energies.

Setting your bindrune in the center of the grid, start to place each respective crystal at all the points surrounding it. As you place the crystals one by one, visualize their energies vibrating in high

universal frequency. Then, imagine this energy being absorbed into your bindrune as you complete the outer circle.

After you have placed all the stones, look at your activation grid. Envision your crystals glowing with power, and from each one, imagine your bindrune drawing all this energy into itself.

You can now leave your activation grid for as long as you desire to let the crystals energize your amulet. You will know when the time is right.

LAW OF ATTRACTION ACTIVATION

In more recent years, the Law of Attraction has taken the world by storm. In its simplest explanation, the Law of Attraction is a philosophy suggesting that our thoughts play a massive factor in our life experiences. Positive and negative thoughts heavily influence what comes into our life, and it is believed that we can manifest whatever we desire by simply **thinking** about it.

Some people have an innate ability to focus their thoughts toward positive outcomes. Still, this will take time, practice, and a certain degree of belief that our desires can be manifested into a reality for many others.

Studies have found that we can each have more than six thousand thoughts in a single day. Just the thought of this alone can nearly give you a headache. However, each of these thousands of cognitive ideas is broadcast outward into the universe in the form of energy. This is why many people believe we can use our thoughts to manifest change in our lives and the world around us.

For example, back when I was in college, I experimented to see how powerful my thoughts were in affecting the world around me. It was quite a simple experiment that involved planting three identical seeds.

As a quick synopsis, I planted three peas in identical containers. The conditions for each one were controlled so that there were no discrepancies. They all had the same amount of soil, water, and light each day. The only variable in this experiment was the thoughts that I would be projecting to each pea.

I lined up the three containers side by side on a tray near a window. The first pea on the left was given positive, uplifting, and 'good' thoughts. The middle pea was left alone to grow naturally without any interference. The pea on the right was given negative, horrible, and 'bad' thoughts.

After about a month or so, the peas started to grow, except for the one on the right. At first, I did not want to believe that my thoughts could have made that much of an impact, but I was pleasantly surprised.

The outcome after my experiment astonished me. The first pea on the left, which was given good thoughts, had grown to be about 2 inches high. It was solid and beautiful, just like the thoughts that I had given it. The middle pea, which was left alone, had grown to be about half the size of the first one. Finally, the last pea on the right, which was given negative and awful thoughts, had not broken the soil.

I was curious as to why the last pea had not made an appearance because I thought it would at least start to grow but may have been a little stunted or shorter than the rest.

Out of curiosity, I dug up the last seed and what I found utterly blew my mind. The one seed that I had given bad and negative thoughts to was completely rotten in the soil.

As you can see, our thoughts play an enormous factor in the world we live in and how we can affect and change our current realities. This being the most paramount reason you must focus your thoughts throughout the entire bindrune process.

Regarding activating your bindrune, you can accomplish this by focusing your thoughts on what you intend to manifest. You can energize your amulet by holding it, speaking to it, and giving it positive, uplifting, and inspiring thoughts that reflect the desire you wish to achieve.

You can also activate your amulet by carrying it with you when you are engaged in an activity that brings you joy. If that means going for a walk, or going to the beach, bring your bindrune with you so that it can take in natural energy from the world around you while you are in a happy state of mind.

SPELL OR CHANT ACTIVATION

Another form of activation that many practitioners highly revere is to use spells or chants. Spells and chants offer us a more focused means of directing our energies and thoughts using words that reflect our intentions.

As with most aspects of magic and spellwork, it is solely up to you how you choose to write them. A spell is essentially a poem directed outward to the universe to empower and mirror our intentions. Your spell does not have to rhyme, although it does sound a lot fancier and magical when it does.

If you prefer to cast a protective circle before reading your spell, do what you feel is necessary. Then, when you think the time is right, say your spell out loud and follow your usual practice to finish the activation ritual.

 When you are writing your spell, pay close attention to the words that you will be using. Each word on its own will have a profound effect on the outcome of your magical workings.

 For instance, if you are activating a bind rune intended to bring you more money and prosperity, I would avoid using the word 'debt' in any circumstance. Even if you use the word in a sentence such as, "I wish to be free from debt," or "I am now debt-free," the universe is still seeing or hearing the word debt and the vibrational command to bring you more.

 The word debt is hard to emotionally override as there are so many negative connotations associated with it. Additionally, if you were to use the phrase, "I am now debt-free," the vibrations of the word's debt and free and energetically opposite therefore canceling each other out, giving this phrase little to no impact anyway.

 A better re-phrasing of this affirmation would be something like, "I am now financially free," or "I am now living a life full of abundance." Like I mentioned earlier, the way we word our spells will determine whether they will be successful or not.

 When activating my bindrunes, I tend to keep my spells or chants short and to the point. They do not need to be long and drawn out unless, of course, this is how you prefer to practice.

 Here is an example of a short spell that works for my activations. Feel free to use this spell if you wish or change the words to match your intent.

*"Strong of thoughts and desires through,
Grant me this, my intentions true.
Universe grant my heart's desire,
By power of Earth, Air, Water, and Fire.
As I will it, so mote it be."*

If you wish to chant your activation, you must choose one or two words that reflect what you are trying to manifest.

If you are trying to manifest abundance in the form of financial freedom, you can use the word 'money.' If you are trying to attract a lover into your life, you can simply use the word 'love.'

When you are chanting, focus your thoughts on achieving what it is you want, and believe that it has already come to fruition in your life.

Holding your bindrune in your hands, repeat your chosen words repeatedly, becoming more and more passionate and louder as you say them in succession. At the end of your chant, you will essentially be yelling your words to the sky for the universe to hear.

It may make you feel a little silly or foolish, but if you want something that bad in your life, you will do almost anything to make sure that the universe is listening, right? And try not to take yourself so seriously anyway. The Gods and Goddesses have a sense of humor too, so if you fart in the middle of your chant, just laugh it off and continue.

Believe in yourself and believe in the magick you have within you. You choose the way to practice your craft. Know that the magick comes from inside you, and there is no need to be embarrassed about it. You can always practice in private and away from judgment or prying eyes to help you focus better.

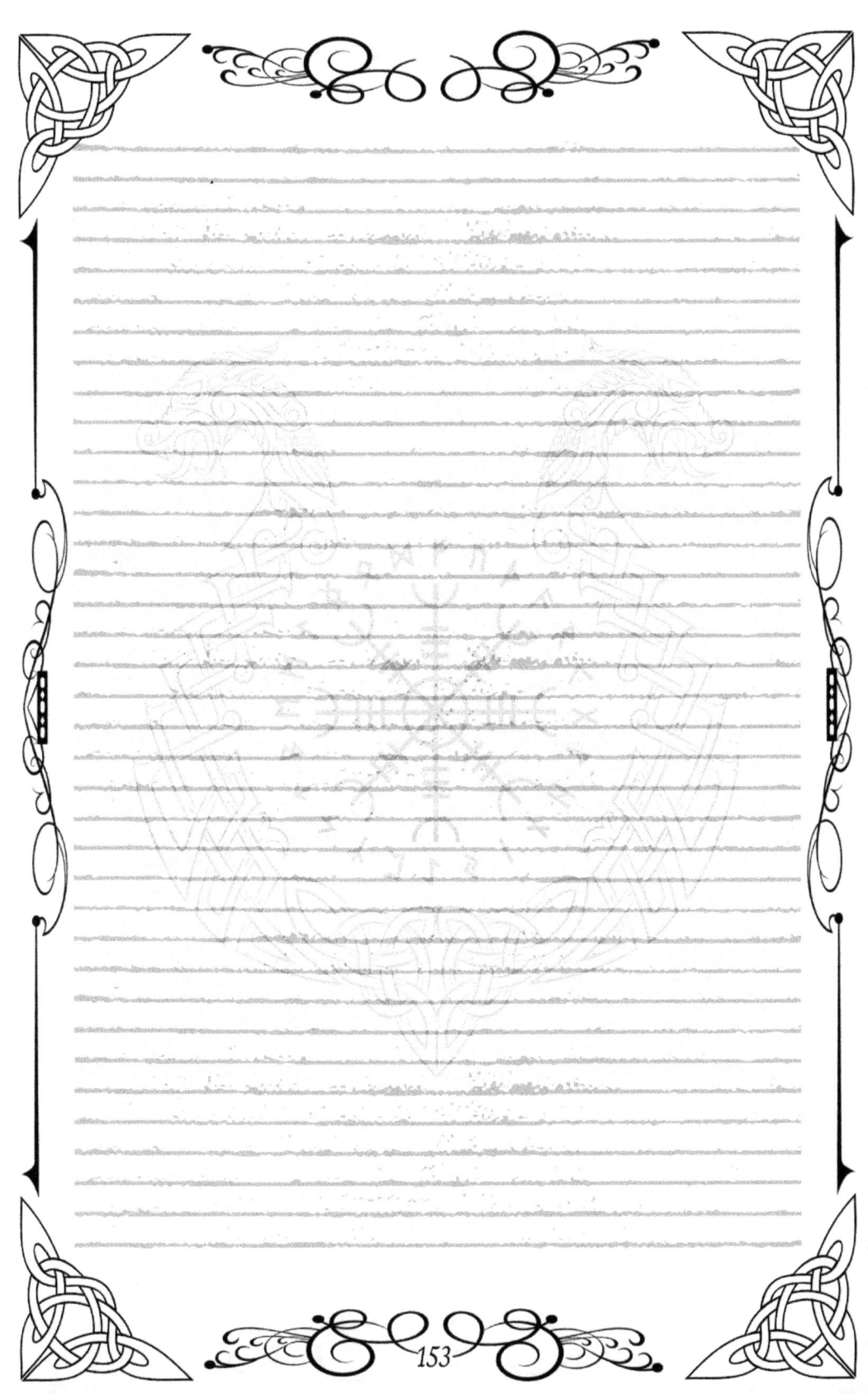

Using your Bindrune

> *"Ask for what you want and be prepared to get it."*
> – Maya Angelou

After you have created and activated your bindrune, what do you do now? Your bindrune is now your focal point for your manifesting going forward.

You have now dedicated so much time and energy toward creating your bindrune, building it, and activating it. I am sure you are thinking and hoping that something will come of it, right?

You will need to determine how and where you would like to utilize your new amulet for manifesting your desires. Depending on what you created the bindrune for, whether to manifest more abundance and money, attracting a special love, or protection, you need to place it somewhere that you will see it every day.

Keeping this bindrune in the forefront of your mind and thoughts every day will help to empower the intentions you set upon it. What is the primary focus for your bindrune?

If you are trying to manifest more success professionally, consider placing your amulet somewhere in your office or taped onto your computer screen.

If you are trying to manifest more money, wealth, or abundance, consider placing your bindrune in your wallet or purse if it is small enough.

If you are trying to manifest protection in your everyday life, consider placing your bindrune in your home or maybe in your car for protection while you travel.

No matter where you decide to place it, seeing it every day will remind you of the intentions you set and keep your energetic vibrations in tune with the universe to help manifest those desires. Keep your bindrune for as long as you require or need it. However, once you have accomplished or manifested your goals, you can choose to destroy your bindrune. Since your dreams have been realized, the bindrune is no longer the center of energy for your intentions. Therefore, it is no longer needed.

If you choose to destroy your amulet, I suggest doing it in a way that you can return the energies to the universe and earth. This can be done through a ritualized burning, burying it deep within the ground, or if it is heavy enough, let it rest at the bottom of a lake, ocean or river.

The method that you choose is entirely up to you. You can also lock it away in a jewelry box, and when you need an extra dose of gratitude, take out your bindrune and remember how grateful you felt when your manifesting came into reality for you.

Whichever method you deem appropriate, please do not forget to thank the universe for granting your desires and bringing a positive change into your life.

Conclusion

 Bindrunes provide a unique magickal practice. Above all else, being more of a magickal process than ritualized magick where there is a definite start and stop in a dedicated 'ritual space.'

 Creating a focal point that endures is generated through the process of creating a bindrune. This dominant focus can persist for days, weeks, months, or even years. How long this continues is entirely up to the creator, their intentions, and the ability to maintain the energy of the bindrunes' physical representation.

 Beginners with a basic knowledge of the runes can create powerful bindrunes or amulets, as there is no need to go through years of in-depth study, obtain complicated materials, or have a large amount of prep time available to practice this magick.

 Bindrunes are not overly complicated to create, and almost anyone can bind a few runes together, place them on a piece of paper or other material, and be done with it.

 Learning more than just the mechanics of building a bindrune will be required if you truly wish to 'get good' at this magickal process. Yes, practice makes perfect, but this will be all for not if the focus is not there.

 The magick genuinely happens when we have what it takes to focus our will and intent on the entire creation of the bindrune from start to finish. These basic steps in manifesting our desires may seem like a leap of faith, but these small actions cause the events we want to happen to come to fruition.

 Your bindrune is an enormously powerful talisman that has been imbued with all your hopes and dreams. You are putting your absolute trust and reverence into this symbol because it is a sign to the Gods

and Goddesses, showing them that you are taking action for what you truly want in your life, and they will pay attention.

We cannot expect to receive any help or guidance from the universe if we cannot help ourselves. Therefore, we need to be responsible and take the necessary actions to start the process of bringing more joy and happiness into our realities. When we can achieve this, the universe and deities will reply.

I hope that you have enjoyed the process of learning and creating your very first bindrune. May this book find a home among its friends in your library and bring you many more years of enlightenment and guidance.

Best of luck on your magickal journey.

In light and love — Blessed Be.

"To live your greatest life, you must first become a leader within yourself. Take charge of your life, begin attracting and manifesting all that you desire in life."
- Sonia Ricotti

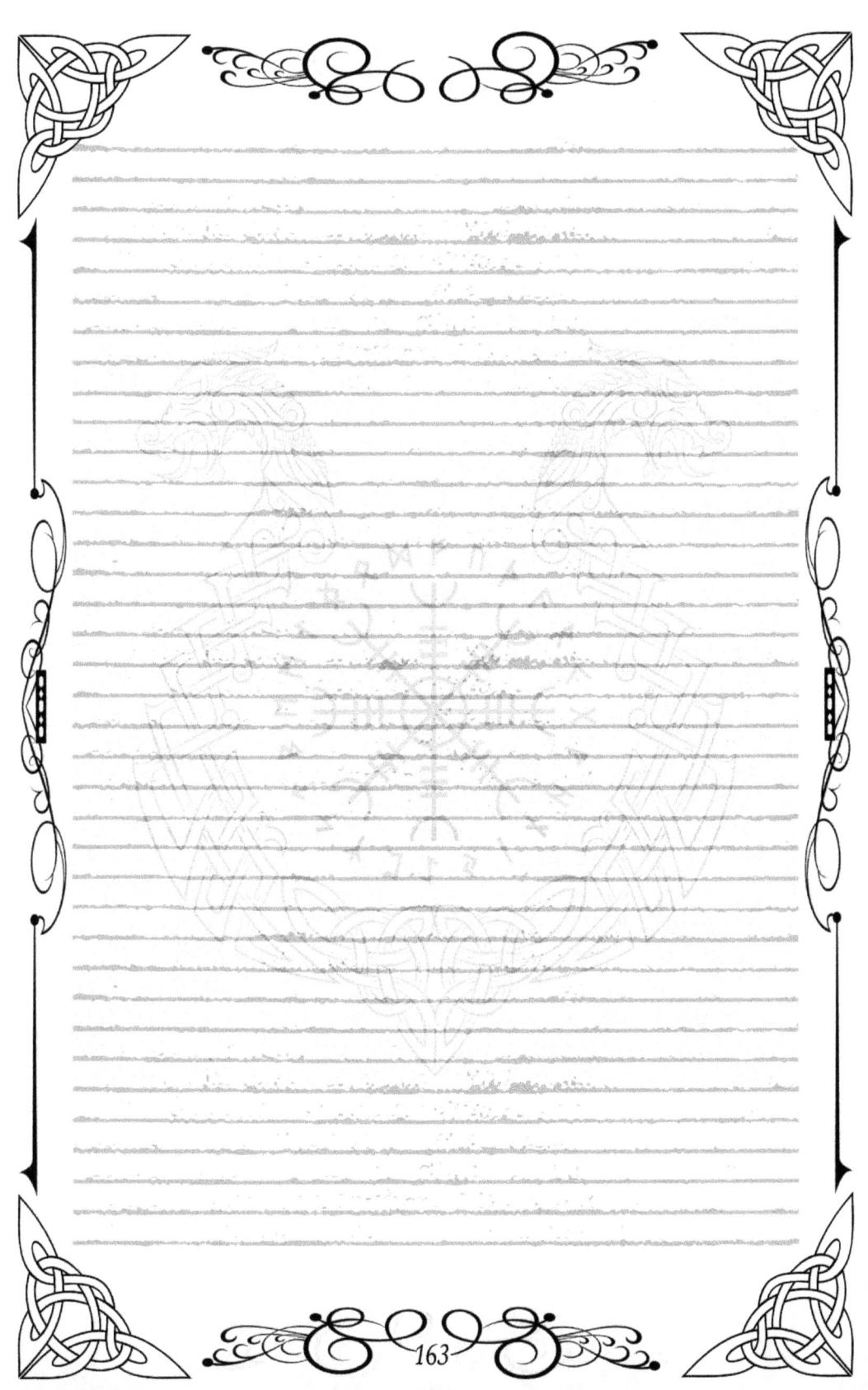

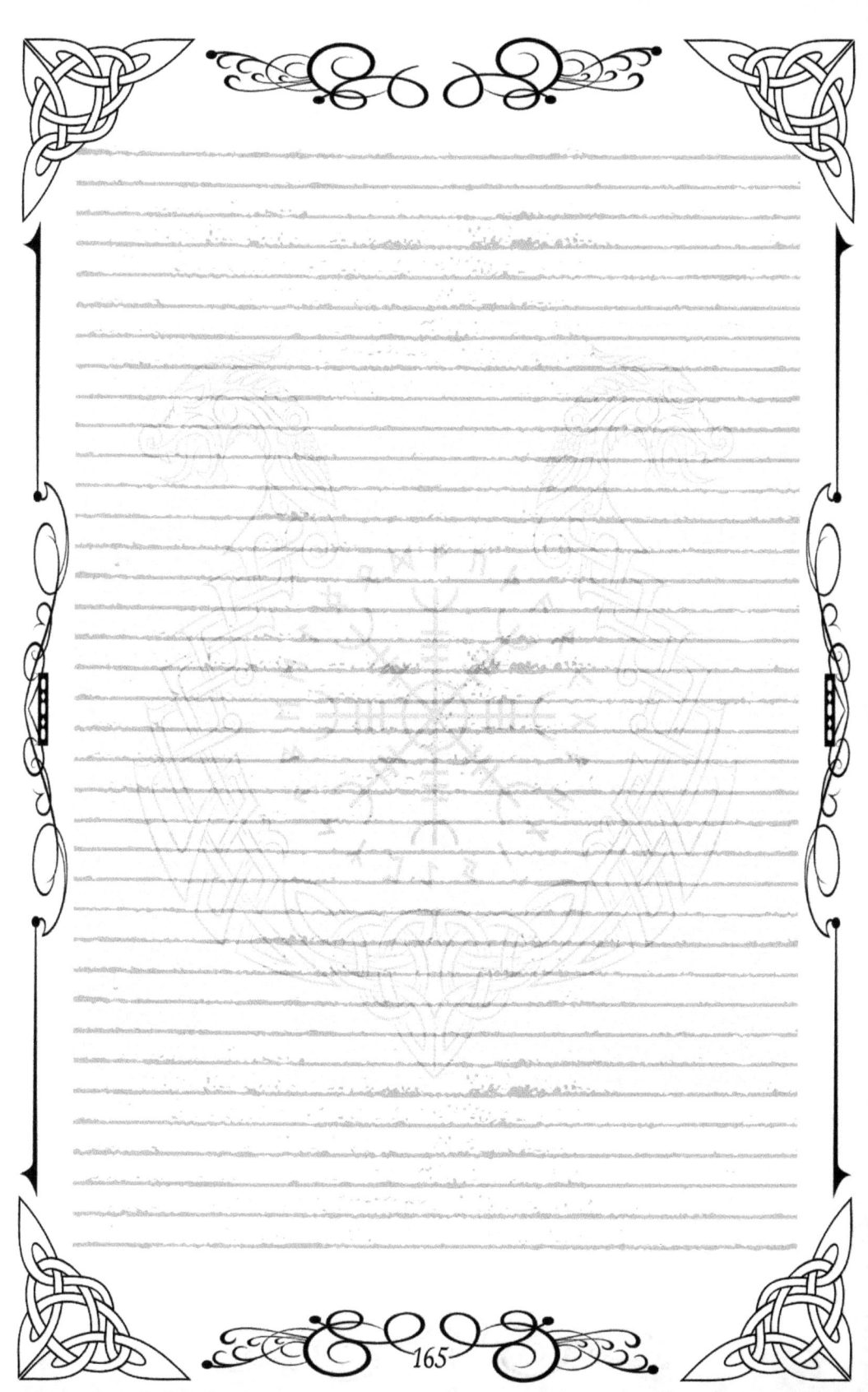

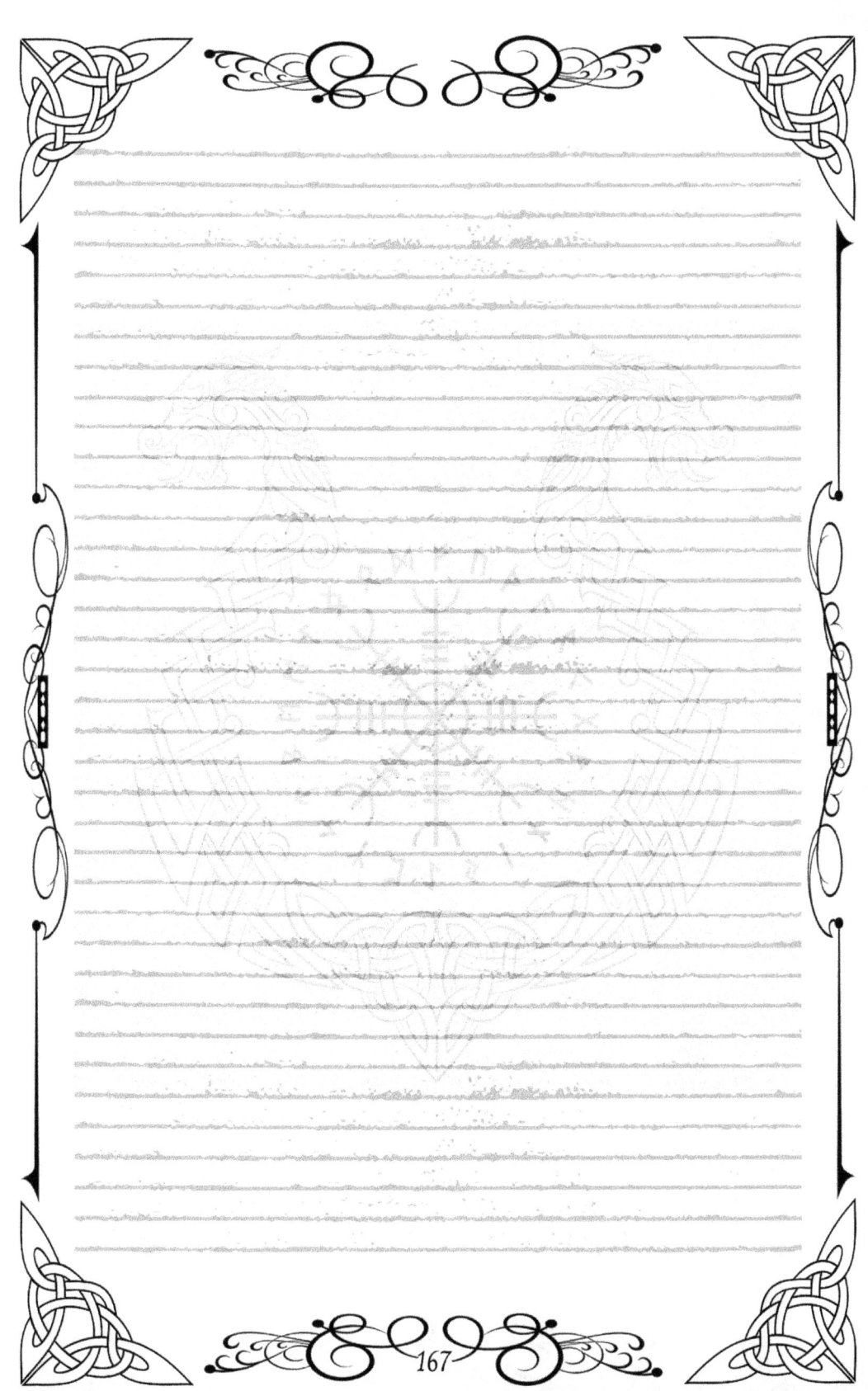

Can you read what the runes are saying in this image?

*ANSWER ON NEXT PAGE

HIDDEN & REVERSED RUNES SOLUTIONS

HIDDEN RUNES

- Urus or Uruz
- Isa
- Mannaz
- Raido or Raidho
- Eywas
- Ehwaz
- Kanu or Kenaz
- Algiz
- Laguz
- Gebo
- Teiwaz
- Daegaz or Dagaz
- Hagall or Hagalaz

REVERSED RUNES

- Urus or Uruz
- Raido or Raidho
- Kanu or Kenaz
- Wunjo
- Teiwaz
- Ehwaz
- Laguz
- Thurisaz

RUNE TRANSLATION

Not all who wander are lost

MORE BOOKS BY J.C. MARCO
AVAILABLE ON AMAZON

ATTITUDE OF GRATITUDE JOURNAL
My Daily Journal of Gratitude & Appreciation

- Features a 30-Day Gratitude Challenge to help kick-start your daily gratitude practice to manifest everything you desire.
- Plenty of blank pages to continue your gratitude journey.

WITCHCRAFT FOR BEGINNERS:
A Practical 2-in-1 Book of Shadows & Grimoire for the New Witch

- Beautifully designed, and boasting over 500 pages, this book is a great start for the beginning practitioner.
- Over 40 different topics covering everything from Crystal and Moon Magick, to Angel Numbers and Cleansing practices.
- Plenty of note pages to record information as you learn about magick and forge your own path.

ABUNDANCE CHEQUES:
Your Personal Manifesting Account with the Universal Bank of Abundance & Gratitude

- Take your manifesting to a whole new level with this full color Abundance Cheques book with Instructions.
- Featuring over 140 blank Abundance Cheques in 9 breathtaking designs.

TAROT READINGS:
A Beginners Journal for Basic Layouts, Recording Readings & Learning Interpretations

- Record your readings while learning your cards meanings.
- Blank templates provided for 105 Single Card Readings and 52 three card readings.
- Keep all your readings in one place!

SOURCES

10 Must-Have Crystals. (n.d.). Hibiscus Moon. https://hibiscusmooncrystalacademy.com/10-must-have-crystals/

Amanda. (n.d.). Elder Futhark Rune Symbols, Meanings and Uses. The Peculiar Brunette. https://www.thepeculiarbrunette.com/rune-symbols-meanings-and-uses/

Aeron. (2015). Bind Runes: A How-To. Aeron's Den. https://aeronsrunestones.tumblr.com/post/12745715 5615/bind-runes-a-how-to

AskAstrology. (n.d.). Zodiac Signs. https://askastrology.com/zodiac-signs/

Beyer, C. (2019, June 5). The Five Element Symbols of Fire, Water, Air, Earth, Spirit. Learn Religions. https://www.learnreligions.com/elemental-symbols-4122788

Bind Rune. (n.d.). Wikipedia. https://en.wikipedia.org/wiki/Bind_rune

Blane, M. (2013). 5 Element Correspondences. Https://Www.Qigong-for-Life.Com/Wp/Content/Uploads/2016/01/5-Element/Correspondences-1-2013.Pdf. https://www.qigong- 173 for-life.com/wp-content/uploads/2016/01/5- Element-Correspondences-1-2013.pdf

Cover Media. (2020, July 20). New study reveals just how many thoughts we have each day. Newshub. https://www.newshub.co.nz/home/lifestyle/2020/07/ new-study-reveals-just-how-many-thoughts-we-have-each-day.html

Creative Commons — Attribution-ShareAlike 3.0 Unported — CC BY-SA 3.0. (n.d.). Creative Commons. Retrieved March 19, 2021, from https://creativecommons.org/licenses/by-sa/3.0/

Crystals for the element of spirit. (2010). Shamans Crystal. https://www.shamanscrystal.co.uk/page/element/spirit/

Elemental Correspondences. (2021). The Hallowed Path. https://www.thehallowedpath.co.uk/elemental-correspondences.html

Elements & Correspondences. (n.d.). By Land, Sea and Sky. https://thenewpagan.wordpress.com/elements-correspondences/

The Five Elements (Wu Xing). (n.d.). Travel China Guide. https://www.travelchinaguide.com/intro/astrology/fi ve-elements.htm

Harreira - Everything Pirates. (n.d.). Harreira. https://harreira.com/symbol/what-do-the-runes-around-the-helm-of-awe-mean/

Home of Chiji. (2020, March 9). Crystal Gifts for Every Zodiac Sign. Chiji. 174 https://homeofchiji.com/blogs/news/crystals-for-every-zodiac-sign

SOURCES

Into the Woods. (n.d.). McCormick Wands. https://www.mccormickwands.com/into-the-woods

The Magic of Fabrics. (n.d.). Marjolijn Makes. https://marjolijnmakes.com/writings/essays/the-magic-of-fabrics/

Mckay, A. (2020, August 21). Viking Runes: The Historic Writing Systems of Northern Europe. Life in Norway.https://www.lifeinnorway.net/viking/runes/#:~:text=The%20first%20%C3%A6tt%20lost %20the,%2C%20j%2C%20z%20and%20s.

MME FORMTASTICA. (2020, August 31). Top 10 Crystals for Beginners. House of Formlab. https://houseofformlab.com/top-10-crystals-for-beginners/

Mohnkern. (2008, May 11). Introduction to Bind Runes. The Modern Heathen. http://www.modernheathen.com/2009/04/16/introdu ction-to-rune-staves/

Morrissey, M. (2020, October 5). 31 Spiritual Law of Attraction Quotes to Transform Your Life. Brave Thinking Institute. https://www.bravethinkinginstitute.com/blog/life-transformation/spiritual-law-attraction-quotes

Mosher, B. (n.d.). The Five Elements. Mosher Health. https://www.mosherhealth.com/mosher-health-system/chinese-medicine/yin-yang/five elements#:~:text=The%20basic%20elements%20ar e%20wood,they%20need%20to%20be%20balanced .

Prout, S. (2015, November 21). 7 Steps to Setting Powerful Intentions. Sarah Prout. https://sarahprout.com/7- steps-to-setting-powerful-intentions/#:~:text=Intention%20setting%20is%20t he%20first,Attraction%20can%20work%20her%20 magic.

Representing the Elements with Crystals. (2018, March 12). Flying the Hedge. https://www.flyingthehedge.com/2018/03/representi ng-elements-with-crystals.html

Rune Magic 101: What are and how to make Bind Runes. (2021). Time Nomads. https://www.timenomads.com/rune-magic-101- what-are-and-how-to-make-norse-bind-runes/

Runes. (n.d.). Wikipedia. https://en.wikipedia.org/wiki/Runes#:~:text=The%2 0earliest%20known%20sequential%20listing,Kylve r%20Stone%20in%20Gotland%2C%20Sweden.

Runes, Alphabet of Mystery. (n.d.). Sunnyway. https://www.sunnyway.com/runes/meanings.html

Shine, T. (n.d.). A Beginner's Guide to Clearing, Cleansing, and Charging Crystals. Healthline. https://www.healthline.com/health/how-to-cleanse-crystals#overview

Shutterstock. (2021, March 15). Shutterstock License Agreement(s). https://www.shutterstock.com/license 176 Skjalden. (n.d.).

SOURCES

Skjalden. https://skjalden.com/why-is-bluetooth-called-bluetooth/

Sons of Vikings. (n.d.). Sons of Vikings. https://sonsofvikings.com/blogs/history/viking-runes-guide-runic-alphabet-meanings-nordic-celtic-letters

Tamane, A. (2020, April 29). How to Create a Bind Rune. Green Moon. https://greenmoon.ca/blogs/blog/how-to-create-a-bindrune

Top 10 Healing Crystals for Beginners (and Their Powerful Benefits). (n.d.). Desert Citizen. https://desertcitizen.com/blogs/style/top-10-healing-crystals-for-beginners-and-their-benefits

Witches Tools: Trees Correspondence. (n.d.). Sacred Hands Coven. https://sacredhandscoven.wordpress.com/2014/08/16/witches-tools-trees-correspondence/

Zodiac. (n.d.). Witchcraft & Wizardry The Age of Grindelwald. http://wandw.wikidot.com/zodiac#:~:text=Associate d%20Things,-Colors&text=Traditional%20Woods%3A%20Oak%20and%20Holly,as%20a%20favorable%20wand %20wood.

Zodiac Signs and Astrology Signs Meanings and Characteristics. (n.d.). Astrology Zodiac Signs. https://www.astrology-zodiac-signs.com/zodiac-signs/cancer/